Celebrating the Kingdom!

The King's Passover

Restoring the Season of Our Deliverance in the Kingdom Lifestyle of God's People

Pastor Deborah Munson

Published by Springs of Shiloh Ministries
6528 Shepherd Rd
Shepherd MT 59079

ISBN: 978-0-578-87543-9

Dedication

To my amazing husband, Tim, who supports and encourages me at every turn in the road of our amazing journey together. Of all the gifts God has given to me, you are the greatest! Thank you for your unconditional and unwavering love...and for giving me endless moments of joy and laughter. Life would be so dull without you!

To my children and grandchildren, who are the greatest blessings and rewards in my life! You are in my prayers every day. May this book become a meaningful part of my legacy to you. May your hunger to know more of our Creator, YHVH, and His Truth always be the passion of your hearts and minds. He makes himself known to those who diligently seek Him. Never stop being a seeker!

Acknowledgements

Gratitude, respect, and honor are words of action that are especially important to me! Life is not a one-man, or a one-woman, show. The best things in life flow from family, friendships, and persons committed to seeing each other succeed in the purpose and vision God has given to them.

This book is a labor of love for me. From the time my husband and I experienced our first Passover Seder to the weeks of work it took to bring order to my years of exploring, studying, and practicing this important celebration in God's Kingdom, these pages cover a span of decades. Our first Seders took place when our children were young, and we knew little concerning what we were doing and why. We simply knew that if Jesus celebrated Passover, we probably should check it out.

Over time we lost the practice. A trip to Israel in 2009 rekindled that old flame. Now our children are grown, with children of their own. They have witnessed their parents' understanding of faith in the Messiah and the way that we live our lives in His Kingdom shift dramatically over the last 12 years. Passover has become a big deal to us, as have the seventh-day Sabbath and the other of YHVH's Feast Days. I am grateful that they have honored us in this journey. They have taken the time to learn from us and to participate… and that has meant a great deal to my husband and me. Thank you, children!

I wish to acknowledge those who, apart from our immediate family, have played a significant part in our journey out of the traditions and doctrines of men and back to Messiah's Kingdom, based on the

Word of God and the One who spoke it. Never have we felt so free…and so at home with Him! To each of these below, thank you for the significant role you fill in helping me reach for God's best my life.

- ❖ Dr. Suuqiina: My friend, brother, and mentor on this incredible path of finding freedom, joy, and truth in the Hebrew roots of our faith in Yeshua. He has inspired me to never abandon my identity.
- ❖ Richard and Barbara Kirchhevel: Wonderful friends that, back in the 1980's, first introduced us to seeing our Savior through Hebrew eyes.
- ❖ Our faith family at Union of Christians Church in St. Petersburg Russia: Our four years with them sparked our deep hunger to know and understand the Kingdom of God and how it functions on earth
- ❖ Kathleen Neff: My friend, sister, and mentor who has encouraged my journey into the deeper things of Messiah and His Kingdom.
- ❖ Priscilla Williams – My friend, sister, and fellow minister who invited us to take our first trip to Israel, which forever changed our lives.
- ❖ Eran Salamon – My friend and favorite tour guide in Israel through whom God revealed to me how much I did not know or understand of His Word, His Land, and His People.
- ❖ Pastors Steve & Evelyn Heimbichner – Our pastors, friends, and companions in this journey to learn and experience all that we can in our relationships with the Lion of Judah, the King of Israel.

I also want to acknowledge and honor my parents and my grandparents who brought me up with a love for God and a passion for our Lord and Savior. I am indebted especially to my maternal Grandma Katie and my paternal Grandpa Frank for letting me know before they left this world that much of my physical heritage and identity is in Israel. Though our families are strong Christians, my ancestors were Jewish … and this I must never forget.

Most of all, I want to thank my King and Messiah, Yeshua, for never giving up on me! With the constant flow of His deep and mighty River of Life ebbing through my being, He has gently guided me all my life through every dark valley, over every challenging mountain, and across every refreshing meadow. The One that I love so very much has taught me the wonder of simply dwelling in His Presence. Without Him, I am nothing.

Deborah Munson, 2021

Table of Contents

Dedication iii

Acknowledgements v

Introduction: Keys to Understanding God's Kingdom.............1

Chapter One: First Things First 27

Chapter Two: Passover and the Week of Passover...................43

Chapter Three: Yeshua's Passover 59

Chapter Four: Passover in the Apostles and Prophets.............83

Chapter Five: Preparing the Heart and Home for Passover ...99

Conclusion: Passover is Something We Live.......................117

Bonus #1:   A Daily Guide to the Passover Season............121

Bonus #2:   A Hebrew Passover Seder Haggadah for
Followers of Yeshua 139

Bonus #3:   Mashiach's Feast for Messianic Believers........183

About the Author 197

Note: All Scripture references and quotes contained in this book are from the <u>Complete Jewish Bible</u>, translated by David H. Stern, Jewish New Testament Publications, Clarksville, Maryland, 1998.

Introduction:
Keys to Understanding God's Kingdom

The Good News of the Kingdom

As a Christian of many years, the question that once perplexed me was "What is the Kingdom of God?" The writers of the New Testament accounts of the life of Yeshua (Jesus) tell us that the Messiah spent his years in ministry traveling from place to place healing the afflicted and teaching the Good News of the Kingdom of God. Obviously, this Kingdom was important to Him. Most English translations of the New Testament render the phrase *good news* as *the gospel*. Most Evangelicals equate the gospel to be the death and resurrection of Jesus Christ and our acceptance of him as our Savior and Lord. But when Yeshua went around teaching the Good News of the Kingdom of God, He had not yet died, nor had He been resurrected. What then was He teaching to the people? What was this news of the Kingdom of God that was so incredibly good?

That questioning led me to even more questions. If the Kingdom is such Good News, why didn't I know more about it? I knew that I have salvation and have eternal life in Yeshua (Jesus) and am to adapt myself to walk in His character, yet I sensed there was something more to this Kingdom thing. Going to church and singing hymns, listening to Bible stories and good sermons, then going home to be a good person and live a good life was all fine and dandy. But was this it? Is it possible that God's Kingdom has a pattern of living that we are to establish on earth as it is in heaven? Is there a daily reality to His Kingdom that has become shrouded in religion and western civilization? If God's Kingdom is indeed eternal, then what does it look like without all our present familiar forms and functions of daily life? Quite frankly, if the world I live in suddenly collapsed would I still know how to live in God's Kingdom?

When I began to discover and understand that the Kingdom of YHVH (God's name) is just like any other kingdom, the keys to living in that Kingdom "on earth as it is in heaven" began to open doors in my Father's house for me that I had never anticipated. Imagine how taken back I was when I realized that the whole concept of a *good kingdom* that man has tried to establish in various forms of governments and nations throughout millennia has its roots in the original great kingdom of the universe – the Kingdom of YHVH. I realized that it is in our God-designed human nature to want to have a good kingdom to live in! We were created in His image – and He is indeed the King of His Kingdom. Our inner beings long to be restored to His Kingdom. Unfortunately, we all too often want the loving and grace-filled King that He is, but not His Kingdom and the accountability to Him that comes with it. Hence, world history is filled with the many futile attempts of man to create kingdoms and governments on earth that conform to whatever concept of heaven on earth we can humanly come up with. Certainly, in our times, it seems the less the King of the Universe is involved in our human kingdoms the more we like it. That is until our kingdoms and governments become irrational and start to crumble around us. Then we cry out to the unseen King to save us.

We mortal humans simply are not capable of accomplishing heaven on earth on our own. This reality brings me to a key Kingdom of YHVH revelation. Yeshua came to rescue us not just from our personal sin, but from a confused & wandering life in the manmade religious and corrupt civil kingdoms of this world. As important as personal salvation is – and it is especially important - His purpose for our salvation goes far beyond having a relationship with him and escaping eternal death. The purpose of Messiah's death and resurrection was indeed to make us worthy to return to our Creator and enter His Kingdom again. His grace and our atonement come no other way. However, the teaching ministry of Messiah had another great purpose: to instruct us on how to live in His Kingdom again. To do this, He repeatedly took his listeners back to the Word of God – back to the Torah – and revealed God's heart imbedded in the instructions and principles given there. *He kept calling them home to the Kingdom. He is calling us as well.*

What is Yeshua's Good News? The Father's Kingdom is *now*, and it is fully accessible! We can return to God's abundant life found there. The way home is simple. Repent. Humble oneself, admit failure, and return to God's Ways. The time has come to stop twisting God's Word to fit human desires and ideas of righteousness. Part of His mission was and still is to set things straight again. Therefore Yeshua kept telling them that the Kingdom was not far removed from them. It is here. It is now. It is only a breath – a confession and a change of heart – away from them. And soon it would be so for all the world, not just the Jews. That was the Good News – and it remains Good News!

What so many of us fail to grasp is that the Messiah of the cross and the empty tomb is exactly what He said He was. He is the threshold (door, gate) to entering the Father's Household, His Kingdom. It is our starting place. When we step across the Threshold, we have stepped into the entry way of our Father's House. Once inside, we discover that we have a great deal to learn and to adapt to. We have been saved not so we can continue to live our lives any way we want to, but to be made worthy of living by the higher ways of His Kingdom. From that moment of salvation, we acknowledge that we are to no longer live by the ways of the world's confused kingdoms. Our lives become a journey of renewing our minds and learning how to live abundantly in our Father's Kingdom, a life for which we were designed and created. We are free from the world's bondages to live our life fully in Him and in His Kingdom of blessings, favor, and abundance. We are not free from living as a citizen of His Kingdom and a child of His Household is to live. His Kingdom, His Household, is one of peace, order, and pleasantness. We are to learn how to honor Him by keeping it that way. Our behavior changes. His does not!

Messiah's Kingdom teachings, which are challenging to our fallen and selfish nature, give us a strong understanding that an abundant and blessed life in His Kingdom is only possible through allowing God's Word and the presence in our lives of His Holy Spirit to change the way we think and live. We are to adapt our lifestyles to His Ways…not the other way around. To stop at the cross and never move into the numerous chambers of His Royal Household is like stepping though the door of your earthly father's house, but never going past the main entrance. If you stay at the door, you will never enjoy the food at His table, recline on the comfy sofa in His living room, rest peacefully in the place He prepared for you, or enjoy the abundance He has stored to meet your every need. Worse yet, you will not learn of the beauty of your Father's character and might. Until you step past the entry point and into His Abiding Place you will never fully grasp the wonderful life that he has for you because *it is only in those inner rooms of His House where mysteries are revealed, and blessings can be given to you.* Thank God for the cross and the empty tomb of Yeshua! But it is time, beloved child of God, to step deeper into His House, His Kingdom. There is so much more waiting for you!

Our purpose in this book is not to go into all the wonderful truths and details regarding the Kingdom of YHVH. Please, be encouraged to dig deeper into Scripture on these things! For now, it will be enough simply to summarize the major points of the Kingdom. Gaining a kingdom mentality starts with understanding that every kingdom shares key features that, as I stated earlier, derive their origin from YHVH's original and eternal Kingdom. This will be important to keep in mind as you begin to process what the King's Passover holds for you. The key features to every kingdom are:

- **Every Kingdom has a King.** He may appoint others to represent him, but his sovereignty is final. His decrees and covenants bind even him to his word. He cannot break his word and remain a good and proper king.

- **Every Kingdom has a People.** The citizens are either natural citizens (natural branches, natural children) or legalized citizens (grafted-in branches, adopted children). The citizens of a kingdom are granted rights and privileges by the will and decree of the king. The children of the king are provided an inheritance by the will of the king.

- **Every Kingdom has a Land** with geographic boundaries established and protected by the king. The king sees to it that this Land holds and produces all that is needed to provide for and nobly sustain his citizens in their labor and services.

- **Every Kingdom has Law** (standards, principles, and instructions) that protects and guides its citizens. Set standards, principles, and instructions are established by the king in a constitution. This constitution is the foundation of the government of the kingdom and guides what is to be allowed and not allowed in the realm of the king (laws). The kingdom's system of justice is based upon its constitution. A kingdom has judges who represent the king's voice and authority and must judge as determined by the constitution of the kingdom.

- **Every Kingdom has an official Language.** A common kingdom language keeps communication clear and daily life consistent. A kingdom's language will carry meanings and idioms that only a citizen will grasp.

- **Every Kingdom has a Culture.** A culture consists of customs, morals, environment, education, and a common belief system and lifestyle. Some of these things are shaped by the laws of the Kingdom and the decrees of the king. Others will be shaped by the characteristics and nature of the land in which a kingdom exists. A kingdom's culture (and language) gives it a unique identify among the kingdoms that surround it.

- **Every Kingdom has a Calendar.** This calendar sets in motion how the times and seasons of a kingdom are observed and greatly determines how life is conducted daily, weekly, monthly, and annually. A kingdom's calendar is marked with celebrations declared by the king and enjoyed by its citizens. These festivities help to keep the identity of the citizens intact and give the king opportunities easily to interact and dwell with the citizens. A kingdom's calendar is essential to ensuring a healthy ebb and flow of life in the realm.

Key Point: None of the above can be removed from a kingdom without creating confusion and weakening its relevance in daily life. Without all seven firmly in place the foundation is weakened and, if not restored, will result in the collapse of a kingdom – or a nation. (Did you know that in Hebrew the number 7 signifies *completeness, order, and stability*?)

With these seven features of a strong, healthy kingdom in hand, let's consider how God's Kingdom is built according to His decrees and creative goodness. (Note: You will find all these features recorded for our benefit in the Torah which consists of the first five books of the Bible: Genesis, Exodus, Leviticus, Numbers, and Deuteronomy. The Torah is called *D'var Elohim*, the Word of God.)

- **The Kingdom of YHVH has a King** – Yeshua the Messiah, is the eternal King over God's Kingdom on the earth and in heaven. Yeshua existed before the foundations of the earth were formed and is one with YHVH, the Father. In and through Yeshua, all things are created. By the act of Creation, His Supreme Sovereignty (Kingship) over all that is seen and unseen is fully established. His complete authority is witnessed in His ability to grant authority on earth to humankind. (Genesis 1:1-30, Exodus 15:18, Deuteronomy 6:4, Isaiah 37:16, Psalm 10:16, 2 Chronicles 20:6, John 1:1-3; 10: 30 & 38; 17:11 & 22, I Corinthians 8:6, Colossians 1:16, and Revelation 19:11-16)

- **The Kingdom of YHVH has a People**, both natural and "grafted in". Beginning with the descendants of Abraham, Isaac and Jacob, this people on earth is called by the King *the whole House of Israel*. Through Yeshua both Jew and Gentile become One New Man in Him and are citizens of His

Kingdom on earth, the commonwealth of Israel. (Genesis 12:1-3; 15:5-16; 17:1-22, Exodus 19:3-8; 24:1-8, Deuteronomy 29:10-14, Jeremiah 31:31-33, Ezekiel 37:1-28, Matthew 15:24; 28:18-20, John 11:51-52; 17:20-23, Romans 11:1-36, Ephesians 2:11-22, Colossians 3:5-15, Hebrews 8:6-12, Revelation 14:9-12; 15:1-3)

- **The Kingdom of YHVH has a Land.** The land is called Israel and the King has established its boundaries upon the earth. Currently the human-formed state of Israel holds a portion of the land. When Yeshua comes to establish His throne on earth, the land promised by God to Abraham and his descendants will belong to and be occupied by all who are Israel. King Yeshua will rule from Jerusalem, the city of His choosing. (Genesis 12:7; 13:14-16; 15:117-20, Deuteronomy 31:23, Joshua 1:1-10, Isaiah 66:20, Jeremiah 16:14-16; 30:1-11; 31:1-26, Ezekiel 11:13-21, Amos 9:11-15, Joel 3:14-17, Micah 4:1-7, Psalm 48, Matthew 5:34-35, Revelation 20:1-9)

- **The Kingdom of YHVH has Law** established and given by the King of the Universe. Adam and Eve were the first of mankind to rule over the earth with YHVH to establish His Realm and His Ways on earth as in heaven. Adam and Eve failed the King (and themselves), but they did not forget His Ways. YHVH attempted to re-establish Kingdom order and law through Noah in hope that all of mankind from that point would benefit. Again, mankind failed. Now the King of the Universe would focus His efforts by assigning His Kingdom purposes on earth to one family. Abraham and His descendants became chosen and destined by YHVH to become a nation of His priests and kings on earth on His behalf. First, He wrote His Ten Words, the constitution of

His Kingdom on earth, upon tablets of stone at Mount Sinai. Then through the writing skills of Moses, He restored in written form all the wisdom and knowledge of His Kingdom that had been lost or abandoned by humankind since Adam. Moses, Aaron, and then Joshua taught the King's instruction to his people who were now called Israel. (Keep in mind that Israel did not have a human king for 400 years after they entered the Land. Legal and moral issues, rebellions against God's Ways, and wars with surrounding nations were dealt with by prophets and judges that the King appointed to represent Him. Until Samuel anointed Saul, YHVH was their only King, and His Word their only constitution and laws.) Through Messiah and the giving of His Spirit to His people, YHVH has fulfilled His promise of a better Covenant for His People by writing His Torah upon the hearts and minds of those who have chosen to return to His Kingdom. Yeshua made a permanent and single way for all mankind to return to Him and re-enter His wise and grace-filled Realm. Through His Word, with His Spirit teaching and empowering us, we can once again learn how to live on *earth as it is heaven.* (Deuteronomy 10:1-13:5, Psalm 119, Jeremiah 31:31-33, Matthew 5:17-20, John 8:55-59; 14:22-24, Acts 24:14-16, Ephesians 5:1-16, Colossians 3:1-11, Hebrews 8:8-12, Revelation 19:11-13)

• **The Kingdom of YHVH has a Language.** That language is Hebrew. The Hebrew language is filled with layers of meaning and contains cultural expressions (idioms) that unlock deep truths about the King and our relationship to Him. Every letter of the Hebrew alphabet has a phonetic sound, is a picture, holds a numerical value, and has a musical value. This makes God's Word and the teachings of Yeshua a many-layered treasure full of meaning and revelation beyond measure. Those who know the language and its cultural uses hold keys of understanding that others do not. (Exodus 3:13-15. God spoke His name to Moses in Hebrew. Genesis – Deuteronomy is God's Word, the Torah, spoken to and recorded by Moses in Hebrew. All the Old Testament books are written in Hebrew. Many of the New Testament books were first written in Hebrew. These New Testament manuscripts were recently discovered hidden deep within the vaults of the Vatican.)

- **The Kingdom of YHVH has a Culture.** The Kingdom of God on earth has a culture that has grown out of the Torah and the Land in which many of His people live. The culture of His Kingdom separates His people from the nations and systems of the world around them. Those cultural elements that the King has firmly established by His Word are unchangeable, eternal, and to be honored no matter where on earth the people of His great Kingdom live. (The Torah: Genesis – Deuteronomy. This culture is supported and documented by the Writings, the Prophets and Revelation, the teachings and lifestyle of Yeshua, the Acts of the Apostles, and the letters written by Apostles.)

- **The Kingdom of YHVH has a Calendar set by the King.** His Calendar establishes days, weeks, months, and a year. His Calendar has Appointed Times of celebration and remembrance that bring His citizens into His presence. They are His Feast Days. These Appointed Times help us remember who we are and who He is. The Appointed Times of the King point us forward to our magnificent destiny with the Messiah. YHVH's calendar separates us, His People, from the rest of the world's systems of gods and pagan rituals. They help us retain our history and culture. They remind us of what YHVH has done, is doing, and will do for us. They hold everything that is good and amazing about our relationship with Him. The King's Calendar establishes on earth the rhythm of life in His universe and His Kingdom in Heaven. His People delight in walking in step with that royal rhythm! (Genesis 2:1-3, Exodus 12:1-13:16, Leviticus 23, Numbers 28:1-29:40, Deuteronomy 16, Isaiah 66:15-24, Zechariah 14:8-21)

The King, His People, the Land, the Law of the Kingdom (the Torah), the Language, the Customs and Lifestyle, and the King's Calendar are all *one package*! Remove any of these elements and the Kingdom of YHVH upon the earth is thrown into confusion and opens itself to infiltration, deceptions, and rebellion. Remove the Torah and His Kingdom loses its power and effectiveness. Each person begins to do what is right in his or her own eyes, adapting to the religious and cultural traditions of other nations and people groups, thus losing their clear identity with the Kingdom. Such become pagan – meaning lost, confused, and without God.

Father calls these His prodigal sons, the lost sheep of His pasture, those who have become like foreigners living outside of His Kingdom and estranged from His Ways. It is these "lost sheep of the House of Israel" that Yeshua came to seek out and make a way of return…be it Jew or Gentile! We must grasp that our salvation in Him is far more than personal deliverance. It is meant to be a return to the Kingdom of YHVH and the adventure of learning again how to live in that Kingdom on the earth. The King has written His Word on our hearts and minds. His Kingdom is within us! The Good

News is that once we have returned, He can help us discover His Truth and re-establish His Kingdom on earth. The first step is to make Yeshua not only Savior but our KING. What our awesome KING instructs, we do…not because we must, but because we love Him so much that we want to!

One of the first areas of returning to God's Kingdom Ways that most of us can grasp and begin to live by is a return to the King's Calendar through honoring and celebrating His Feast Days. Notice that they are called HIS Feast Days, HIS designated times. They are not Jewish. *They are His.* (Leviticus 23:2 & 4, Exodus 12:11, Isaiah 66:22-23, Zechariah 14:16-19) He appointed them to be honored and enjoyed by all who belong to His Kingdom. They were established for us as a reflection of what exists in heaven. Through them, He reveals to us the full nature of His character and His plan to redeem all mankind and His creation. The Feast Days bring a little taste of heaven to our life on earth! They are nothing less than remarkable!

The King's Calendar

The calendar of God's Kingdom as it operates on earth serves marvelous purposes. First, it reveals YHVH's direct relationship to the time and seasons He established on the earth and how He desires to relate to us through them. Scripture teaches us that all the heavens and the earth were created by Him and belong to Him. The first two chapters of Genesis tell us that Father YHVH created the sun, moon, and stars, setting them in place and putting our universe in motion. He tells us that He established these celestial forms as signs of His times and seasons. Using them, YHVH established for us night and day, weeks, months, seasons, and years. His design is that through them He can provide the blessings of rest and celebration to man, and refreshment to the earth and all its creatures. In giving us seasons of planting and harvest He supplies provision and abundance for man. In the context of relationship, YHVH is our Father King who has established a regular cycle of provision and blessing for His children. When we step out of that cycle, we lose out on both.

Second, after the fall of man YHVH also began to use the times and seasons to communicate to us signs of warning. He does not hesitate to cause deviations in the regular rhythm of the times and seasons for this purpose. For example, deviations such as too much rain or heat at the wrong time or in the wrong season can have life altering effects. Creator will cause this as a judgment against a nation. (By biblical pattern, judgments sent by God are usually intended to provide a path to deliverance and opportunity to return.) The times and the seasons on earth are an active and powerful means of communication between Father YHVH and His people. Certainly, we would all agree that every form of communication is a crucial key in any relationship!

Third, the times and seasons help us to know where we are in relationship to the Second Coming of Messiah. Yeshua chastised the religious leaders of His day for knowing how to read the sky in regard to the weather, but not being able to understand or read the signs of the times they were living in. If they had chosen to pay attention to the spirit of season they were in and embraced the meaning in the signs of that season, they would have embraced Him immediately. Yeshua also told His disciples that many would not recognize the signs of the coming of the Bridegroom and thus not be prepared. Therefore, we should probably take His words to the religious folk of His day to heart. We too need to be wise and know the times and the seasons around us. It is by His design that we will know His return is eminent, and the manner in which He will return, simply by paying attention to and learning from the times and seasons of God: His Feast Days.

Our modern Western civilization has become far removed from understanding and living in rhythm with the times and seasons of the earth. This is especially true concerning those things that are strongly related to the sun, moon, and stars. Electricity makes us less concerned about the darkness of the night. We can function and work straight through to sunrise. We have flashlights rather than only the light of the moon to illuminate our path. We have motorized vehicles that make travel by night or day no big deal, any time of the year. Modern architecture, energy technology, and transportation keep us insulated from the effects of the seasons. In fact, the seasons have become a nuisance to us, rather than a blessing from YHVH. We are frustrated by delays in our plans and disruptions in our travel. We complain about such things as road closures and shoveling snow covered sidewalks. Our ancestors not that far back had to live *with* the seasons. These days, we are determined to live *despite* the seasons, resenting the characteristics of each for intruding on our plans. Most of us no longer concern ourselves with reading the skies to understand anything going on around us. It is a tragedy that what YHVH has set in the sky and in the changing of seasons to give testimony of His greatness and to communicate with us is now so easily and largely ignored.

I am not talking about astrology or the worship of nature here. I am talking about living in knowledge and awareness of what Elohim (Creator God) placed into motion in His Creation to help us know Him and understand how He desires us to relate to Him and to each other. According to His ways and wisdom, there truly are times and seasons for everything under the sun. (Ecclesiastes 3:1)

Prophetically, we know Messiah and the prophets tell us that there will be signs in the sky regarding the sun, moon and stars that will alert us to events about to take place, including His return. It may be a good idea to pause and reconsider how we presently relate to the natural times and seasons established by the King of the Universe, and how well we are aware of what is so brilliantly spread over us in the sky both day and night. They are there for our benefit; to bless us when all is in right relationship with Him, to warn us when all is not right, and to help us prepare for the coming of our Groom.

Before we go into the Feast Seasons and specifically the celebration of Passover, it is good to be aware of how YHVH has crafted into His universe days, nights, weeks, and months. Briefly,

- **A day** is defined as sunset to sunset. This is based on how God defined a day to Moses in the first chapter of Genesis. "There was evening and there was morning, the first day"... and this is repeated for all the six days of creation and the Sabbath. (Genesis 1)

- **A week** is defined by God as seven days, with six days to labor and the seventh day designated as *Shabbat* – the Sabbath. In the Hebrew language the six days are called by number, not names. Only the seventh day has a name; Shabbat meaning *rest*. This day was given not only to mankind, but to all creation, including the land on the earth. (Genesis 2:1-3) *Shabbat is foundational to the Creator and is to be honored as the first and most important of His Appointed Times.* Yeshua declared himself to be Lord (Master) of Shabbat and kept it without fail during his life on earth. We are to be like Him in all things.

- **A month** is defined by the phases of the moon. Each new month is marked by the appearance of a new moon after the night of no moon. YHVH established that a celebration be held on the first day of every new month. This is known as *Rosh Chodesh*, meaning *head of the month*. In some Bible translations, this celebration is also called a New Moon festival or celebration. Isaiah 66 informs us that Rosh Chodesh will carry into the new heaven and new earth during Messiah's 1000-year earthly reign, as will Shabbat and all His Feast Days. (Numbers 10:10; 28:11-15, I Chronicles 23:30-31, 2 Chronicles 8:12-13; 31:3, Psalms 81:3, Nehemiah 10:32-33, Isaiah 66:22-23)

The lunar month causes a great deal of confusion for us westerners with our solar-based calendar handed down to us by Rome. When we start to give serious attention to the King's Feast Days it seems that they are bouncing all over the place from year to year. Rest assured, they are not! On His Calendar they take place on the same dates every year. On a lunar calendar the months are shorter that on a solar calendar. Thus, the days and dates will not match calendar to calendar. It does take a few years to adjust one's thinking to simply accepting the King's Calendar over the western world's Gregorian calendar and choose primarily to function accordingly. Even in modern Israel it is impossible not to pay attention to both calendars – a necessity if one is to interact with the rest of the world. However, in His Kingdom *our life is to be timed to the rhythm to the King's Calendar* and when His Feast Days arrive the western calendar is to take a firm second place. Our lives conform to His Ways...the King and His Kingdom do not conform to the worlds' ways. Period.

There are two major feast seasons in the Kingdom Calendar, both related to seasons of harvest. The first contains **the Spring Feasts** and is referred to as *the Season of Our Deliverance*. The second is **the Fall Feasts** and is referred to as *the Season of Our Joy*.

The Spring Feasts celebrate the spring harvest, primarily the crops of barley and wheat. The Fall Feasts celebrate the autumn harvest when the abundance of the land fully comes in. The Spring Feasts include Passover, the Feast of Unleavened Bread, and the Day of First Fruits. Also included is Pentecost, which takes place 49 days after the Day of First Fruits and is aligned by God with the wheat harvest in Israel. The harvest connection to the Feast Seasons is to teach us that as His people we are to be harvest-minded; always aware of the principles of sowing and reaping, seed time and harvest.

The Fall Feasts include The Day of Trumpets (Shofars), the Day of Atonement (for the nation of Israel), and the Feast of Tabernacles. Both sets of Feast Seasons hold historical, present-day, and prophetic significance. They are not things of the past. They are very much *here and now...*and *yet to come*. They remain truly relevant and should be extremely important to the Bride of Messiah, both Jew and Gentile as one People in Him.

From this point forward, we are going to focus on the celebration of Passover, the first of the Spring Feasts. This incredible celebration takes place in the first month of the Kingdom year and sets into motion seven days of deeply meaningful celebration. As with any celebration that is set to go on for a week, there is a great deal of preparation to be done. The King has given some specific directions in the preparation for and the celebration of Passover. He also graciously allows us to use His creative nature within us to carry them out. With all this in mind we are going to start building our understanding of Passover with the first day of the month in which it takes place, the month of Aviv. This will help us place the amazing Feast of Passover in its full context.

Israel and the Church

Before we move on from here, I want to address an issue that is probably coming to mind right now. What is the relationship between Israel and the church? If the Feast Days are for Israel, why should the church bother with them? I ask a question in return! Are you willing to consider that, in God's perspective, His Kingdom is not to be divided? According to Paul, they most certainly are not. Let me give you a hint! There are two things the early church did not have. They did not have a New Testament. They did not have a church.

Rather, as Paul teaches, those of Israel that accepted Yeshua as the Messiah and King were to keep studying the Tanakh and attending synagogue. The Tanakh is what we call the Old Testament. In the teachings of Yeshua and the writings of the apostles, the Tanakh is referred to as the Scriptures. The first attempts at compiling what would be called the New Testament took place around 200 AD. The New Testament as we know it was created in the 6th century AD. In the first century church everything taught regarding Yeshua's life and teachings rested upon gaining a sound understanding of the Tanakh. A perfect example of this is found in Paul's letter to Timothy.

> But you, continue in what you have learned and have become convinced of, recalling the people from whom you learned it; and recalling too how from childhood you have known the Holy Scriptures (Tanakh), which can give you the wisdom that leads to deliverance through trusting in Yeshua the Messiah. All Scripture

(Tanakh) is God-breathed and is valuable for teaching the truth, convicting of sin, correcting faults and training in right living; thus anyone who belongs to God may be fully equipped for every good work. 2 Timothy 3:14-17

The word *synagogue* is the Hebrew term for *a place of assembly*, with the function of worship and teaching in the community of faith. The Greek word for such a place of assembly is *ecclesia* and is translated *church.* When the New Testament writings were translated into common vernaculars, the word *synagogue* was used to describe any assembly that was definitively Jewish. The word *church* was used to describe any assembly that had to do with those who followed Yeshua, regardless of if they were Jew or Gentile. This was done with great intention, for by this time Replacement Theology had taken its hold in the Church. The worlds of Jew and Gentile, even within the Body of Messiah, were not allowed to touch each other. However, in the first century church, up until the time Christians were expelled from the synagogues, there was an expectation among the leaders that both Jewish and Gentile believers would be able to learn of Messiah's ways (the Torah) by faithful attendance in the Jewish assemblies. This is found in the book of Acts in the context of a special meeting, or council, held by the apostles and elders in Jerusalem over issues that had arisen due to the influx of Gentiles that were now coming into the faith of Abraham, Isaac, Jacob, Moses, and Yeshua. Until Peter and Paul had experienced the tremendous response of God- fearing, God-seeking Gentiles to the Good News of Yeshua and the Kingdom, the "church" was almost entirely Jewish! Arguments had broken out as to how these Gentiles were to conduct their lives in Messiah. The council's discussions and ruling includes an eye-catching phrase that we need to pay attention to.

Then the whole assembly kept still as they listened to Bar-Nabba (Barnabas) and Sha'ul (Paul) tell what signs and miracles God had done through them among the Gentiles.

Ya`akov (Jacob, the Hebrew name belonging to James) broke the silence to reply. "Brothers," he said, "hear what I have to say. Shim`on (Simon Peter) has told in detail what God did when he first began to show his concern for taking from among the Goyim a people to bear his name. And the words of the Prophets are in complete harmony with this for it is written, 'After this, I will return; and I will rebuild the fallen tent of David. I will rebuild its ruins, I will restore it, so that the rest of mankind may seek the Lord, that is, all the Goyim who have been called by my name,' says Adonai, who is doing these things. All this has been known for ages.

Therefore, my opinion is that we should not put obstacles (such as undergoing physical circumcision) in the way of the Goyim (people of the nations, Gentiles) who are turning to God. Instead, we should write them a letter telling them to abstain from things polluted by idols (idolatry), from fornication (sexual impurity), from what is strangled and from blood (unclean diet). <u>For from the earliest times, Moshe (Moses) has had in every city those who proclaim him, with his words being read in the synagogues every Shabbat (Sabbath).</u>" **Acts 15:12-21**

The early church leaders made it clear that those coming to faith in YHVH through the Messiah were to learn the Torah (Moses) by going to the synagogues every Shabbat to listen to the reading of the Torah! This recalls exactly what Yeshua had instructed His followers.

Then Yeshua addressed the crowds and his talmidim (disicples): "The Torah-teachers (scribes) and the P'rushim (Pharisees)," he said, "sit in the Seat of Moshe (Moses). So whatever they tell you, take care to do it. But don't do what they do, because they talk but don't act!" **Matthew 23:1-3**

The Seat of Moses was a specific location in the synagogue (place of assembly) that was occupied by a leader in the faith every Shabbat. In the Seat of Moses only that week's Torah portion could be read aloud, word for word. No commentary or sermonizing was allowed. Because Torah scrolls were not a common household item, this served as the best means for all to hear the Word of God just as it was recorded by Moses. Thus, Yeshua instructed them: Whatever is spoken from the Seat of Moses, take care to do it! Do as God said, not as these scribes and Pharisees do! (If one reads on in Matthew 23, Yeshua describes the errors of these leaders.) Yeshua was certainly not telling anyone to ignore the Torah, was He?

The writings of Paul and Peter express what the early church came to understand. It had been a mystery at first, but then came the Spirit-given understanding. Contrary to what they had been taught to believe since childhood, a non-Jew was not unclean. He was merely lost without God. What God makes clean through His Word, now written on their hearts and minds by His Spirit, was clean! This was the work of the Messiah. All men and women are to be brought into oneness with God through Messiah. This was the message Yeshua was trying to teach them! This was the Good News of the Kingdom!

In his letters, Paul made this new oneness of Jew and Gentile as clear as he knew how to.

Therefore, remember your former state: you Gentiles by birth— called the Uncircumcised by those who, merely because of an operation on their flesh, are called the Circumcised— at that time

had no Messiah. <u>You were estranged from the national life of</u>
<u>*Isra'el. You were foreigners to the covenants embodying God's*</u>
<u>*promise. You were in this world without hope and without God.*</u>

But now, <u>you who were once far off have been brought near</u>
through the shedding of the Messiah's blood. For he himself is our
shalom—<u>he has made us both one</u> and has broken down the
m'chitzah (divider in the Temple which separated Jew from
Gentile) which divided us by destroying in his own body the
enmity occasioned by the Torah, with its commands set forth in
the form of ordinances. He did this in order to create in union
with himself from the two groups <u>a single new humanity</u> and thus
make shalom (peace), and in order to reconcile to God both in <u>a</u>
<u>*single body*</u> *by being executed on a stake as a criminal and thus in*
himself killing that enmity.

Also, when he came, he announced as Good News shalom to you
far off and shalom to those nearby, news that through him <u>we both</u>
<u>*have access in one Spirit to the Father.*</u> *So then, <u>you are no longer</u>*
<u>*foreigners and strangers. On the contrary, you are fellow-citizens*</u>
<u>*with God's people (Israel) and members of God's family (Israel).*</u>

You have been built on the foundation of the emissaries and the
prophets, with the cornerstone being Yeshua the Messiah himself.
In union with him the whole building is held together, and it is
growing into a holy temple in union with the Lord. Yes, in union
with him, you yourselves are being built together into a spiritual
dwelling-place for God! **Ephesians 2:11-22**

In that case, I say, isn't it that they (the Jews) have stumbled with
the result that they have permanently fallen away?" Heaven
forbid! Quite the contrary, it is by means of their stumbling that

the deliverance has come to the Gentiles, in order to provoke them to jealousy.

Moreover, if their stumbling is bringing riches to the world—that is, if Israel's being placed temporarily in a condition less favored than that of the Gentiles (Ephraim and the nations) is bringing riches to the latter—how much greater riches will Israel in its fullness bring them!

However, to those of you who are Gentiles I say this: since I myself am an emissary sent to the Gentiles, I make known the importance of my work in the hope that somehow I may provoke some of my own people to jealousy and save some of them! For if their casting Yeshua aside means reconciliation for the world, what will their accepting him mean? It will be life from the dead!

Now if the hallah (bread) offered as firstfruits is holy, so is the whole loaf. And if the root is holy, so are the branches. But if some of the branches (of the Olive tree, Israel) were broken off, and <u>you—a wild olive—were grafted in among them and have become equal sharers in the rich root of the olive tree</u> (Israel), then don't boast as if you were better than the branches! However, if you do boast, remember that you are not supporting the root, the root is supporting you.

So you will say, "Branches were broken off so that I might be grafted in."

True, but so what? They were broken off because of their lack of trust. However, you keep your place only because of your trust. So don't be arrogant; on the contrary, be terrified! For if God did not spare the natural branches, he certainly won't spare you!

So take a good look at God's kindness and his severity: on the one hand, severity toward those who fell off; but, on the other hand, God's kindness toward you—provided you maintain yourself in that kindness! Otherwise, you too will be cut off!

Moreover, the others (the Jews outside of Messiah), if they do not persist in their lack of trust, will be grafted in; because God is able to graft them back in.

For if you were cut out of what is by nature a wild olive tree (Ephraim and the nations) and grafted, contrary to nature, into a cultivated olive tree (Israel), how much more will these natural branches be grafted back into their own olive tree (Israel)! **Romans 11:11-22**

What about God, who supplies you with the Spirit and works miracles among you—does he do it because of your legalistic observance of Torah commands or because you trust in what you heard and are faithful to it?

It was the same with Abraham: "He trusted in God and was faithful to him, and that was credited to his account as righteousness."

Be assured, then, that it is those who live by trusting and being faithful who are really children of Abraham. Also, the Tanakh, foreseeing that God would consider the Gentiles righteous when they live by trusting and being faithful, told the Good News to Abraham in advance by saying, "In connection with you, all the Goyim (Gentiles) will be blessed." So then, those who rely on trusting and being faithful are blessed along with Abraham, who trusted and was faithful. **Galatians 3:5-9**

Friend, from God's perspective the believing Jew and the believing Gentile are one! They belong to one olive tree, Israel. They are united through Messiah as one body, a single new humanity. United in the Spirit, all of us have the same access to the Father that Abraham had. Gentiles, you are no longer Gentiles! You were once foreigners and strangers, but now you are a part of God's people (Israel), members of His household. Jews, you are no longer Jews! You were once bound to legalistic observance of the Torah and trapped in the lifeless, loveless rules and traditions your religious leaders created to control you and keep you in fear. No longer! You are free in Messiah to live the abundant life, given by YHVH, to all of us in His Word. You have returned to being the Israel God had originally intended and designed.

Truly, through the seed of Abraham – Yeshua the Messiah, *all* the nations have been blessed! Together, we have become fellow citizens in His Kingdom. We both draw upon and are supported by the rich Root of the Olive Tree. That Root is Yeshua (YHVH Saves), the Living Word of God. Together, we are the restored Whole House of Israel! We are Yeshua's *Netzarim*, His *Little Branches*.

There is not to be separation between Israel and the Church. That is the great deception of Rome that has plagued both for centuries. There is no separation between the Tanakh and the New Testament. They flow seamlessly into one narrative belonging to one King and His Kingdom. This restored House of Israel is the *one* Bride of Messiah, the Word made flesh, who was with God in the beginning *and is God*! (John 1:1-14) Praise God, He is, in our times, bringing the two sticks back to one in His hand. (Ezekiel 37)

The Sabbath (as God defines it) and His Feast Days are for His Kingdom, Israel. Jew or Gentile, if you have entered His Kingdom through Yeshua, His Appointed Times for His people, Israel, are for you. You Groom (your Betrothed Husband) is waiting to spend these times with you. Enter in and enjoy them with all the love in your heart that you have for Him!

Chapter One:
First Things First

Rosh Chodashim -- the Biblical New Year

The Spring Feasts mark the beginning of the King's New Year for his People on earth. Passover, the Feast of Unleavened Bread, and the Day of First Fruits position us with Him to receive an abundance of freedom, blessings, and harvest in the year ahead. YHVH uses the feast days to remind us that our relationship with Him is unique and has a definite past, present and future. At the head of every year, we are given opportunity to reset everything in our lives to our King's times, seasons, and Ways. As we cycle through the King's Feast Days year by year our relationship with Him should become tighter and tighter, increasingly intimate, and increasingly filled with His Light and Life. That is His heart and design for us. What a gracious and loving King we serve!

The observance of Rosh Chodashim (Head of Months) is considered the very first instruction given to the Hebrew people by God as they prepared to leave Egypt to become a nation. Soon they would have a life of freedom from Pharaoh's oppression and Egypt's pagan ways. They were to be given a new beginning. Exodus 12:1-2 reads, *"YHVH spoke to Moshe and Aharon in the land of Egypt, 'You are to begin your calendar with this month; it will be the first month of the year for you.'"* YHVH then gives Moses and Aaron the instructions for the first Passover which took place in Egypt the night before their departure.

This first month of the King's year on earth is known today by two names: Aviv and Nissan (or Nisan). Aviv is the correct Hebrew name and means *spring*. Nissan is the Babylonian name for the same month. Various translations of Scripture will use one or the other. However, the Hebrew text translates the specific use of the name Aviv in Deuteronomy 16:1 which reads, *"Observe the month of Aviv, and keep Pesach (Passover) to YHVH your God; for in the month of Aviv, YHVH your God brought you out of Egypt at night."* Although the modern Jewish calendar calls it the month Nissan, I have chosen to honor the Hebrew name Aviv. Therefore, as I present to you dates for the preparation and celebration of Passover, I will refer to the month as Aviv.

Let's keep first things first by looking at Rosh Chodashim (Head of the Months) and the month of Aviv in a little more detail. Look at that Deuteronomy 16:1 passage again. *"Observe the month of Aviv, and keep Pesach (Passover)..."* Why the distinction regarding the entire month of Aviv? There must be something special about keeping Passover in the context of this first month of the King's Calendar. Is it possible that we need to mark that first day of Aviv on our calendar as something to pay special attention to? Yes! After all, the full picture of a Passover celebration begins in only ten days. If we are to be prepared both spiritually and physically, there is much to give attention to!

The new moon of Aviv is one of the most important new moons of the Hebrew calendar. In Jewish communities, the Shabbat (Sabbath) preceding the new moon of Aviv is called *Shabbat HaKodesh* (The Holy Sabbath) and is one of four special Sabbaths in the year. *Shabbat HaKodesh* begins the period of preparation for Pesach (Passover) which is two weeks away. Extra Scripture readings are a part of the synagogue (assembly) service: Exodus 12:1-20 and

Ezekiel 45:16 - 46:18. For the next two weeks, the entire Kingdom community turns our full attention to preparing our homes and places of worship for the Spring Feasts, especially for the night of Passover.

But what about celebrating the New Year of the Kingdom? This is where being of YHVH's Kingdom and being Jewish bump heads a bit. The rabbinical traditions that have been handed down in the Jewish religion often muddy the waters, which is why Yeshua routinely criticized and confronted the religious leaders of His day. There are two New Year celebrations on the Jewish calendar: Aviv 1 (Rosh Chodashim) and Tishri 1 (Rosh Hoshana – which takes place on Feast of Trumpets). Why two? Over the centuries, Jewish sages teach that there are two orders to creation: a natural order of creation and a supernatural order of creation. Tishri 1/Rosh Hoshana (in the fall) celebrates the natural order of creation, referring to the physical creation of the earth and heavens by YHVH. Aviv 1/Rosh Chodashim celebrates the supernatural order of creation, referring to spiritual re-creation or re-birth. For Jews, they see themselves as re-born as a people of the Covenant of Abraham during Passover and the Exodus. Thus, the Aviv New Year is important but not emphasized with a physical observance. Passover is far more important. Today, most Jews celebrate only one New Year holiday – Rosh Hoshana in the fall on Tishri 1. Their emphasis in the spring is on the week of Passover (which includes three of the Feasts of Yahweh.) The first of Aviv merely marks the beginning of two weeks of intense preparation for this huge and meaningful celebration.

For followers of Yeshua, we understand that our full redemption and rebirth is possible because of Passover, the day on which the Lamb of YHVH was slain to take away the sins of the world and give all nations access to the blessings of YHVH's Covenant with Israel. We honor the fact that God created the heavens, the earth, humankind, and all living things that dwell and exist upon it. However, rather than celebrating Rosh Hoshana as a specific new year, we acknowledge creation as proof of the Kings ultimate sovereignty over all things. Our focus that day goes to Yom Teruah (Day of Shofars/Trumpets) and entering the Fall Feasts season.

Personally, I prefer to celebrate the New Year following YHVH's directive. According to Exodus 12:2, Aviv 1 is the beginning of the year for His people. The choice of observing His New Year is, like most choices that He presents to us, a choice between obedience to man's traditions or obedience to His Voice – His Word. Such choices are, in essence, a test of the heart of His Bride…a test of *my* heart. As the first of Aviv, the Head of Months, approaches I review the past year then look to Him for fresh revelation, direction, and understanding for my life for the next year. I enjoy the day of Rosh Chodashim as a holiday and celebrate joyfully with friends and family by beginning our planning and preparations for *The Season of Our Deliverance* that comes with the arrival of Pesach (Passover). In fact, I can hardly wait for the Feasts of the month of Aviv to arrive!

The Month of Aviv

Giving heed to the instruction that we observe the month of Aviv, it is probably wise to consider and remember why the month of Aviv holds significant meaning and position in the Kingdom and in our lives as the King's People.

- Aviv is the month of Israel's deliverance from Egypt, which marks the restoration of Israel's spiritual identity and the beginning of Israel's national history. When the Hebrew people went into Egypt to survive severe famine under the protection of Joseph, they were merely a household made up of Jacob (Israel), his sons and their families; about 70 people total. Four hundred thirty years later they left Egypt numbered in the millions and set out for the land YHVH had promised to their forefathers. They came into Egypt a family. They were leaving as an ethnic group – an identifiable people - twelve tribes strong with a divine destiny to be YHVH's unique nation of priests and kings. They were to be His Light and a source of blessings to all other nations.

- Aviv marks the Biblical beginning of the annual cycle of the Appointed Times of YHVH. Passover is the first in this cycle of seven feasts, broken into three pilgrimages: Passover, Pentecost, and the Feast of Tabernacles.

- Aviv begins a new weekly Shabbat cycle and a new cycle of a year of Rosh Chodesh celebrations.

- Historically, the marking of the number of years of the reign of a King of Israel begins with Aviv 1. As each Aviv 1 passed, one year would be counted to a king's reign. Coronation of a new king of Israel always took place on Aviv 10, the same day of the selection of the Passover lambs and Yeshua's Triumphal Entry into Jerusalem.

Aviv is a month of celebrating deliverance and redemption! Under Moses, Israel was delivered and redeemed out of bondage in Egypt. Yeshua's death and resurrection took place in the month of Aviv during the eight-day period of time given to the celebration of the feasts of Passover, Unleavened Bread and Day of First Fruits. In fact, Yeshua died and was buried according to the timing of Pesach (Passover), remained buried during the first day of the Feast of

Unleavened Bread, and was resurrected on the Day of First Fruits. He completely fulfilled the prophetic picture of God's plan of redemption woven into the Spring Feasts. (He will do the same regarding the prophetic picture of the completion of God's plan of redemption found in the Fall Feasts.)

In this month of Aviv, Yeshua provided for us complete deliverance and redemption from our bondages to the systems of this world and the godless life it traps us in. During this Season of Our Deliverance the penalty for our failure to keep His Ways – our sin – was taken care of. All a person must do is humbly agree with God regarding those failures, ask for forgiveness, receive a fresh start, and step back into His Kingdom Ways with a pure, fresh start! For followers of Yeshua, the month of Aviv holds reason for the greatest of rejoicing and celebration.

Gaining a Hebrew Perspective

As my husband and I stepped into honoring our King by celebrating His Feast Days, we encountered a need to change our mindset. Having both grown up in strong American Christian homes, the Feast Days run a great deal counterculture to what we were used to. The first major shift we had to make was from thinking like an American Christian to thinking like a biblical Hebrew. We had to begin to shift our mindset.

As if it were not challenging enough to embrace a whole new set of holy celebrations, we also had to deal with issues like determining what is of man's religious traditions and what did YHVH really tell us to do. Then we came face-to-face with a rather critical conflict between religious form and Spirit-focused function. It did not take long before we realized that this was going to become a life-altering journey for us. What I am about to share will be crucial to your ability to truly step into the meaning and purposes found not only in Passover, but also in Shabbat and all His Holy Days. Once you grasp these key perspectives, you will find incredible joy and a new intimacy with Messiah that you may have never known before!

The first key perspective is Function over Form. YHVH's Feast Days are not about holding annual festivals just for the sake of doing them. They are not to become religious observances laden with weighty traditions required to methodically move our way through. That, my friend is FORM. As you discover the things required by YHVH in each of His Feasts you might be surprised as to their simplicity, and by the room our Father has left for us to be creative and to enjoy these times within the context of our host cultures and locations. (More about that later!)

Rather than focus on Form, our Father desires for us to focus on FUNCTION. YHVH's *mo'edim* (appointed times, celebrations, rehearsals) are about *the restoration of relationship between Himself and His people.* This is His heart for us in all His Kingdom celebrations, including the Sabbath. He desires to dwell with us in an atmosphere of unity. These special occasions are designed for His People to come together in unity with one another, then experiencing His awesome Presence dwelling with a unified us. This union, or unity, is the heartbeat of our Messiah! It is what He gave His life for. Don't believe me? Read John 17 ~ the prayer of Yeshua in the Garden of Gethsemane. Everything our Messiah did (and continues to do) for us is to cause us to be one with the Father and one with each other. This is why Yeshua confirmed that the greatest of the commandments is to love YHVH with all of our being and to love one another with as much passion and concern as we love ourselves. It is this passion that drives the function of His Feast Days!

As we celebrate Passover and all His Appointed Times, we must keep front and foremost in our understanding that YHVH has given us these special occasions to completely focus on His goodness, to love Him with all that we are, and to love others as we love ourselves. Thus, during the feast seasons a biblical Hebrew mindset understands and determines to function by five key principles:

1. *YHVH's Feasts are never to be celebrated alone.* They are about YHVH's number one priority: relationships. The feasts are to be spent with Him together *with* our families and our congregations. These celebrations remind us of who we are...and to whom we belong. We all need that!

2. *YHVH's Feasts give us opportunity to welcome our King's presence and dwell with Him.* The feasts allow us time to reflect on our Father's goodness and festively celebrate in His presence, especially within our homes. We make an intentional effort to grasp and enjoy the truth that God is with us! Reading His Word, worshipping, enjoying fellowship with His People, and rejoicing with our families center around honoring His presence with us.

3. *YHVH's Feasts give us opportunity to realign ourselves.* With each Feast, including the Sabbath, we intentionally step out of the throbbing pace of the systems of the world and immerse ourselves into YHVH's timing – the times and seasons of His eternal Kingdom. The historical and prophetic elements of each celebration remind us that YHVH is always acting on His redemptive plan for humankind, and all His creation. These Holy Days remind us that the unseen reality of His Kingdom is far more real than what we see with our human eyes. They cause us to "Be

still (stop striving) and know that I am God, supreme over the nations, supreme over the earth." (Psalm 46:10). During our celebrating, we can realign ourselves with YHVH's reality and renew purpose and vision personally, as a family, and as a congregation.

4. *YHVH's Feasts give parents and grandparents the opportunity to fulfill YHVH's direction for us to teach His Ways to our children and grandchildren.* Each Appointed Time is to be used to instruct our families in the Biblical accounts of God's interaction with his People, Isra'el (us). It is crucial to God's Kingdom on earth to know our history and the faithfulness of the King to those who remain faithful to Him. We are never to forget what YHVH has done for us, from Genesis to today. We are also to remind our families of what YHVH has promised for us in the future. In the busyness of our lives, it is good of our King to establish such times when we can intentionally be focused on teaching our children and grandchildren.

5. *YHVH's Feasts give us special opportunities to give and to care for others.* During all His Appointed Times, Father reminds us to care for the widowed, the orphaned, the poor and the imprisoned with extra effort, meaning *above what we already do.* We also bring extra offerings into His houses of worship, giving our congregations the means to care for us and take the Good News of His Kingdom to the lost in our towns and cities. By our Feast Day offerings, we open a window for our King to release His blessings and favor into our homes and congregations...even into our nations.

The second perspective we need to hold fast to is the avoidance of legalism – the leaven of the Pharisees and Sadducees. Over the centuries Jewish religious leadership developed many traditions and practices that take place during each of the feast seasons. In that process they often lost the heart and Spirit of YHVH in the celebrations (function) and made keeping the feasts difficult and burdensome (form). Often their reason was to make it harder for non-Jews to embrace the faith – the exact opposite of the intent YHVH purposed in His assignment to them to be the light of the world and draw all men unto Him.

One of Yeshua's primary purposes in His life on earth was to tear away these traditions of men and return His people to the purity of the Word of God (D'var Elohim) – the Torah. John tells us that Yeshua is the Word of God made flesh and dwelling among us. (John 1:1-14, 1 John 1:1-4, Revelation 19:11-13) He is the Living Torah and He lived out his human life as such, giving us the perfect example of the Kingdom lifestyle, character, and mindset. His attitude of love and forgiveness flows from the Torah that He gave to Moses at Mount Sinai. When a legalistic perspective is peeled away from our understanding of His Word, we soon discover that His Instructions and Principles (the meaning of the word *Torah*) are full of mercy and grace!

This Man, the Living Torah, has called us to think and live like He did...to love YHVH with all our heart, understanding, thoughts, words, and actions. This is why He instructs, "If you love me, you will keep My commandments." Yeshua was at Mount Sinai, and the words recorded by Moses are His Words...His Principles and Instructions...His Lifestyle...His Torah. Forget "Law" – that is Religious Greek and Religious Jewish thinking, not of a biblical Hebrew mindset. Yeshua constantly charged the Pharisees and

Sadducees with perverting His Word, making burdensome what was meant to be life giving, taking His instruction and turning it into a list of laws impossible to keep. In our observance of His Feast Days, we must be wary not to become guilty of the same! Did He not tell us, "Come to me, all you who are struggling and burdened, and I will give you rest. Take my yoke [my Ways] upon you and learn from me; because I am gentle and humble in heart, and you will find rest for your souls. For my yoke is easy, and my burden is light." (Matthew 11: 28-30, see also Jeremiah 6:16)

As I stated earlier, when we look only at the instructions that YHVH, the King of the Universe, gives in Scripture for each Feast celebration there are only a handful of requirements. As His Beloved Bride – His Queen in training – we obediently *choose* to adjust to His directives. We love Him! We long to dwell with Him. We want to live and to walk in perfect unity with Him. We put all our heartfelt effort into learning his Ways and preparing to reign over the earth with Him when all is perfectly restored to as it was in the beginning. Our Wedding Day is approaching. Honoring and celebrating Messiah's Feasts are our rehearsals as we prepare!

Regarding the Jewish traditions that permeate the Feast celebrations, I encourage you to pray and ask our Father to direct you as you create your family's Feast celebrations. Start with His instructions found in His Word. These are a must. Then weigh by His Spirit the traditions that have developed. Some of man's traditions are worthy of use as they enrich and beautify the Feast experience. But they are not required. Keep in mind that in YHVH's Kingdom there is ample room for creativity and cultural expression. Where you live and the host culture in which you were raised will have a place in your festivities. For instance, the Feast of Tabernacles in Alaska is going to look a lot different than in Australia. That time of year, Alaska is an autumn location and already experiencing winterish weather, while Australia is in a spring location and the abundance of a fall harvest is not available. Only in the land of Israel can you truly celebrate the Feasts like they are described in the Bible. Dates, palm fronds, and pomegranates are native there – but not in Alaska. A little improvising based on your location's climate is okay! The big guideline we must follow in all cultures and locations is to do our best to adhere to what is instructed and avoid assimilating anything of pagan gods into our observances.

With such creative and cultural variances allowed, keep in mind that no two households will celebrate each Feast in the same way– and no two congregations will either. Strongly guard against falling into the religious trap of judging each other over how the Feasts are kept. Preserve and honor God's instructions the best you can and pay attention to the "shadow of things that are coming" that exist in each of them. Remember, the Feasts belong to the body of Messiah. Do not cause division over traditions that in the eternal and big picture of the Kingdom simply do not matter. (Colossians 2:16-17) Keep your focus on the function and purpose of each Feast and do your best to understand what Messiah is revealing of Himself and His Kingdom in them. Rejoice in the Truth you receive as each cycle of Feasts comes around. Remember, these are *celebrations*! Keep your heart purely devoted to the King and to those who join in celebrating with you. You will discover *relationship* in a whole new dimension.

Learn Like a Hebrew

Jewish scholars and teachers have a simple set of questions they keep to the forefront of their minds as they study and present the Word of God. In their simplicity, however, is embedded the intent of achieving profound impact. As we study Passover (and any of God's Appointed Times), keep the following questions foremost in your mind. They will help you to embrace the relational aspect that runs deep at the heart of why our Father the King gave us these special observances.

1. **What have I learned?** (from the Biblical text? from the information presented to me?) State the new knowledge with your own words.

2. **What does it mean?** Move from knowing what you have learned to *understanding.*

3. **Why is this important for my life?** Move from understanding to embracing *wisdom.*

4. **What are the implications for my life?** Move from obtaining understanding and wisdom to beginning to weigh the impact this new knowledge and instruction from YHVH should have in your life.

5. **How do I translate this into practical reality in my day-to-day life?** Now what you have learned is about to get real! Identify what you can do to implement what you have learned. Write down every thought and idea that comes to mind. Then ask your Father, by His Spirit, to help you choose what to implement and what to toss away. (Keep in mind that sometimes understanding an instruction or principle given by YHVH is never well understood until you act upon it. In doing, revelation will come!)

6. **How will I share or teach this to others?** This step usually is best saved until you are living by the new knowledge or

instruction from YHVH that you have embraced. In living in his Truth, knowing and understanding His Truth will increase. In preparing to share or teach what you have learned *and applied*, you now have your sleeves rolled up and are working with Truth to whole new depth. A couple of vital principles to keep in mind: The teacher always learns more than the student. And a teacher of God's Word will be held accountable by him to a higher standard. (Where much is given, much is required.)

Specifically, regarding the King's Appointed Times, also ask and answer (with the help of God's Spirit):

1. **How will I allow celebrating this occasion to help me regain and strengthen a profound sense of awe for YHVH?** What actions will I take during this time to deepen my walk and relationship with the King? What kind of environment do I need to create or find for myself to deepen my sense of being one with Him?

2. **How will I allow this celebration to draw me closer to others that I am united with in Messiah?** What actions will I take during this time to interact with my family and my congregation, intentionally looking to encourage them and increase unity among us?

3. **How will celebrating this occasion help to restore Godly leadership in my home?** What can I do to make my home a place of worship and fill it with the richness of YHVH's Covenant with us? What plans do I have for teaching and modeling the Kingdom Truths that are a part of this celebration to the next generations in my family? In my congregation?

In all of this, I am reminded of what the apostle James (Ya'akov/Jacob) wrote to us. "But someone will say that you have faith and I have actions. Show me this faith of yours without the actions, and will show you my faith by my actions!" (James 2:18) In the Hebrew mindset faith (trust) without actions (obedience) is barren. We say we believe, but our belief – our knowledge – is worthless without *living out* what we claim to know and believe. If we are indeed one with and in the Messiah, we must live by what He has instructed with His own Words and modeled for us with this own life. Yeshua did indeed honor and keep Shabbat (the 7th day Sabbath) and the Feast Days. We are to be like him!

The Feast Days are, in many ways, the King's testing of us. He has given us these occasions of rest and celebration, to be in His presence and to remember all that He has done and is still doing for us. Imagine a King who tests His people with something celebratory and enjoyable?! Yet, they are indeed a test. Therefore, we do need to take them seriously and give thought to what we are doing and why. Don't let them sneak up on you. Get out your calendar. Plan for them! Make room in your life for the abundance that they offer. Make the Feasts a part of your home and your life, not add-on's that you will get to when you show up at church or synagogue for them.

The King is waiting for you! Go ahead. Make Him smile! Make Him laugh with joy!

Chapter Two:
Passover and the Week of Passover

The Season of Our Deliverance

Passover begins the season of the Spring Feasts which is called The Season of Our Deliverance. This annual time begins with the night of Passover on Aviv 14 and concludes with Shavu'ot (Feast of Weeks or Pentecost) on Sivan 6. From a purely Old Testament perspective, during this span of seven weeks we are to remember and celebrate 1) the Passover deliverance of the Hebrew people from bondage in Egypt under the leadership of Moses, 2) the journey to Mount Sinai, and 3) the sealing of Israel as God's holy nation in an eternal covenant with Him through the giving and receiving of the Torah.

For followers of Yeshua, the Season of Our Deliverance also remembers and celebrates the death of YHVH's Passover Lamb, His burial and resurrection, and the sealing of us as God's holy people in eternal covenant with Him through the giving of the Holy Spirit. We will go into greater detail on these things in the next chapter.

In the Hebrew mind, Passover is not complete without Pentecost. The purpose of Israel's deliverance from Egypt was to position her to receive God's Torah. Without the Torah (God's Principles and Instructions), their deliverance would be meaningless. Without the Torah, they would have no way of knowing how to live in their new state of freedom, or in the Land that would be theirs. Thus, the giving of the Torah at Pentecost completed the deliverance that Passover initiated. Their redemption as YHVH's People was complete.

As followers of Yeshua, we experience the same. The deliverance (salvation) that was provided by the death of YHVH's Passover Lamb is completed by the giving of His Holy Spirit, which took place on Pentecost. An amazing prophetic event was fulfilled that day. Rather than being engraved in tablets of stone and then written on animal skins and rolled into scrolls, the Torah was placed by YHVH within His people and written on our hearts. He has indeed forgiven our wickedness and remembers our sins no more! (Jeremiah 31:31-34, Hebrews 8:8-12) Just as He did for the Israelites of the Exodus, Messiah provides both our deliverance and our redemption. However, this time our redemption – the changing of our lives – is empowered by the counsel and teaching of Ruach HaKodesh (Holy Breath, Holy Wind, Holy Spirit, Spirit of Truth) in all things concerning Him and his Word. (John 14:15-26)

Before we move on, I want us to travel forward a few thousand years to modern day Israel. God has not finished with His work with Israel during The Season of Our Deliverance. He is still intent on fulfilling His redemptive plans for all Israel. He still sticks to His calendar and its seasons. His prophets foretold of a day when Israel would once again become a nation. (Isaiah 11:11-13; 14:1-8; 60:1-12, Ezekiel 36:1-37, Jeremiah 16:14-15, Zechariah 10:3-12,, Amos 9:9-15, Hosea 3:4-5) Yeshua told us that this would be a sign to us of His imminent return. (Matthew 24:32-33) It was no coincidence that in 1948, during the Season of Our Deliverance, Israel was reborn as a modern nation! It was no coincidence that in 1967, during the Season of Our Deliverance, Israel was, in the completely miracle-ridden Seven Day War, Israel was reunited with and regained control of Jerusalem! During this season in Israel today, the nation observes Holocaust Day (in remembrance of those lost in Germany and Eastern Europe in the 1930's and 1940's), Memorial Day (honoring all who lost their lives in the establishment of Israel in 1948 and while protecting Israel since), and Independence Day (the day modern Israel became a nation again). In that first Season of Our Deliverance, YHVH brought the descendants of Abraham, Isaac, and Jacob (Israel) out of Egypt and established them as His nation intended for His Appointed Land. Forty years later, Joshua took the children into the promised Appointed Land during the Season of our Deliverance. God brought the descendants of Israel out of the nations of the modern world and, during the Season of Our Deliverance, re-established them as a nation in His Appointed Land. YHVH does nothing outside of His times and seasons!

In the Land and throughout the nations, this time of year continues to hold deep and significant historical meaning to all Israelites. As we see the time of Messiah's arrival to fully restore his Kingdom on earth quickly approaching, The Season of Our Deliverance is a time for all YHVH's people, Jewish and Gentile, to keep watch over Israel, vigilantly interceding for her as the nations around her seek to destroy the people of the modern nation of Israel and those throughout the world who are aligned with her. As the King has promised, most certainly He continues as always to keep special vigil over His People, the Land, and His City, Jerusalem, this time of year.

> *The time the people of Israel lived in Egypt was 430 years. At the end of 430 years to the day, all the divisions of YHVH left the land of Egypt. This was a night when YHVH kept vigil to bring them out of the land of Egypt, and this same night continues to be a night when YHVH keeps vigil for all the people of Israel through all their generations.* **Exodus 12:40-42**

Spiritually, The Season of Our Deliverance is extremely important in the Hebrew faith (beliefs *and* lifestyle) and requires days, even weeks, of focused preparation. The season contains four of the seven major feasts of the King: Pesach (Passover), the Feast of Matzah (Unleavened Bread), Yom HaBikkurim (Day of First Fruits), and Shavu'ot (Pentecost). The first three all take place within an eight-day time frame that, for ease of communication, those of Israel simply refer to as Passover – in Hebrew, Pesach. The week of Passover is then connected to Pentecost by a period of 49 days called The Counting of the Omer. All these celebrations, including the Counting of the Omer, are established by our King in the Torah. If we would but take the time to learn about and understand them, all these celebrations should carry deep meaning to followers of Yeshua. After all, according to Paul, we have been grafted into Israel and have become heirs of the same Covenant and citizens of the same Kingdom. (Romans 11:13-27, Ephesians 2:13-22)

Passover: A Night Unlike Any Other

In Hebrew, the word for Passover is *pesach*. The word *pesach* also means *unblemished lamb* and is derived from the word *pasach* which means *pass over*.

I find it amazing that God wove the meaning of these two Hebrew words together long before this one extraordinary event. The blood of a sacrificed *unblemished lamb* would be smeared upon the doorframes of Hebrew homes so that the household would then be *passed over* by the Angel of Death as it passed through Egypt during the night of the killing the firstborn of men and animals of Egypt. This final act of God's wrath against Egypt bought Israel's freedom and delivered them from bondage. The very next day, they left Egypt behind and stepped into their destiny as a nation. YHVH tells His people this special night is always to be remembered as YHVH's Pesach…YHVH's *Unblemished Lamb*. Yes, that night was, and still is, entirely prophetic!

> *"Here is how you are to eat it (the sacrificed lamb): with your belt fastened, your shoes on your feet and your staff in your hand; and you are to eat it hurriedly. It is YHVH's* Pesach *[unblemished lamb, Passover]. For that night, I will pass through the land of Egypt and kill all the firstborn in the land of Egypt, both men and animals; and I will execute judgment against all the gods of Egypt; I am YHVH. The blood will serve you as a sign marking the houses where you are; when I see the blood, I will pass over [Hebrew:* pasach*] you—when I strike the land of Egypt, the death blow will not strike you. This will be a day for you to remember and celebrate as a festival to YHVH; from generation to generation you are to celebrate it by a perpetual regulation."* **Exodus 12:11-14**

If you are not familiar with the Exodus account of YHVH's deliverance of the Israelites from oppressive slavery in Egypt, take the time to read the account in Exodus 1:1-13:16. This historical event is at front and center in the celebration of the night of Passover and in the death and resurrection of our Messiah. To grasp Passover's full meaning, you will want to be familiar with the Exodus account. In fact, to grasp the full meaning of the events of the coming End Times, you will want to be familiar with it. If you have not read it for a while, refresh yourself now! All that we consider from this point forward rests upon this incredible event.

The Feast of Passover celebrates one remarkable one night in Jewish history…a night on which YHVH continues to keep vigil over the Israelites. The Exodus marks in the mind of every Israelite the historical beginning of their people as a nation. For this reason,

Passover is also called the Feast of Freedom as it specifically memorializes the night when YHVH's faithful obtained their freedom through the blood of an innocent, perfect lamb. They did nothing to deserve their deliverance. They did not go to battle to win it. It was given to them by YHVH as an act of love and grace.

> *For you are a people set apart as holy for YHVH your God. YHVH your God has chosen you out of all the peoples on the face of the earth to be his own unique chosen treasure. YHVH didn't set his heart on you because you numbered more than any other people - on the contrary, you were the fewest of all peoples. Rather it was because YHVH loved you, and because he wanted to keep the oath which he had sworn to your ancestors, that YHVH brought you out with a strong hand and redeemed you from a life of slavery under the hand of Pharaoh king of Egypt. From this you can know that YHVH your God is indeed God, the faithful God, who keeps his covenant and extends grace to those who love him and observe his mitzvot, to a thousand generations.* **Deuteronomy 7:6-9**

We see in the Biblical account that the very first Passover was not to be entered into lightly or without preparation. God had something remarkable planned and it required personal cost, time, and inconvenience to fully enter in. The Hebrew people were about to receive their freedom, but the provision of a sacrifice had to be made. There would be personal cost. The people were instructed that on Aviv 10 they were to select per family a male lamb or goat in its first year and without defect or blemish. This would require time. They had to keep the lamb protected, usually within the home, and inspect it thoroughly until the fourteenth day. This would be an inconvenience. On Aviv 14 the head of each household brought their lamb before an assembly of the entire community where it was sacrificed. Then the blood and the body of the lamb would be taken back to their home. The blood was to be smeared on the two sides and the top of the doorframe of the house in which the family would gather. That night they were to roast and eat the entire lamb or goat...nothing was to be leftover. If their household was too small to consume an entire lamb, two neighboring households could come together.

As if that were not challenging enough, on that very first Passover they would have to eat hurriedly and be fully ready to leave behind everything they knew at a moment's notice. Their belts were to be on, feet shod, and staff in hand. They were to be packed up and ready to leave. God was about to perform *suddenly* for them, and they had to be committed to moving out in faith with Him the moment deliverance was provided. This is the essence of Passover. This is what it means to crossover from a life of bondage into a life of freedom. Death was going to pass over them...and they must be committed and ready to move forward with God, leaving what is familiar far behind.

The following Scriptures provide all YHVH's instructions to Israel regarding the celebration of the night of Passover.

The First Passover
- Exodus 12:3-5 The lamb or kid, a male in its first year and without defect, was to be selected on the tenth day of Aviv; one for each household unless the household was too small. Then a next-door neighbor could share one in proportion to the number of people who would eat it.
- Exodus 12:6 On Aviv 14, before the entire assembly of Isra'el the animals are to be slaughtered at dusk. (Some of the blood would be captured in a bowl and both the blood and the animal returned to the household.)

- Exodus 12:7 The blood of the Pesach sacrifice was to be smeared on the two sides and the top of the doorframe at the entrance of the house in which they would eat the lamb.
- Exodus 12:8-10 The animal must be roasted, not left raw or boiled. It is to be eaten in its entirety; nothing is to remain. If anything does remain it is to be burned up completely by morning.
- Exodus 12:8 The meat is to be eaten with *matzah* (unleavened bread) and *maror* (bitter herbs)
- Exodus 12:11 On the first Pesach night, the meal was to be eaten hurriedly with belts fastened, shoes on, and staffs in the hand.
- Exodus 12:14 The night of Passover and the following day of deliverance were to be remembered and celebrated as a festival to YHVH from generation to generation; this is a never-ending, unchanging decree

After Israel's deliverance from Egypt:

- Leviticus 23:5-6 Passover occurs between sundown and complete darkness on Aviv 14; it is Passover for YHVH. The next morning, on Aviv 15, begins the Feast of Matzah (unleavened bread); this is a Shabbat – a day of rest, offerings, and holy assembly
- Numbers 9:1-5 Gives the account of the second celebration of Passover that took place in the Sinai Desert. For those who were unable to celebrate on Aviv 14 due to uncleanness or traveling abroad, a second Passover (Sheni Pesach) was established by YHVH one month at dusk on the fourteenth day of the second month (Iyar). YHVH considers honoring His Passover to be *essential* for the families of Israel.

- Numbers 9:13 The person who is clean and not traveling abroad on Passover and fails observe it on Aviv 14 was cut off from Israel. He had failed to bring the offering for YHVH at the designated time
- Numbers 9:14 If a foreigner (one not of Israel) is staying with you and wants to observe the Passover with you he is welcome to do so, provided he has entered into God's Covenant with Israel and observes YHVH's Passover according to the instructions for the observance of Passover
- Numbers 28:16 Aviv 14 is YHVH's Passover
- Deuteronomy 16:1-2, 5-6 God instructs Israel that once they enter the Promised Land the sacrifice of the Passover offering (the lamb or kid) is to be made "where YHVH will choose to have his name live" (eventually this will be the Temple in Jerusalem); they will be required to roast the meat and eat it in this place, then return to their homes (tents)
- Deuteronomy 16:3-4 They are not to eat the meat of their sacrifice with any food that has leavening; none of the meat is to be left in the morning; no leavening is to be seen in your homes or in your territory for seven days (Feast of Unleavened Bread which begins the next morning)
- Deuteronomy 16:16-17 Passover and the Feast of Unleavened Bread will be a pilgrimage celebration; all the men of Israel are to appear in the presence of YHVH in the place He chooses (which eventually became the Temple in Jerusalem); the men are not to come empty-handed but prepared to give what each can "in accordance with the blessing YHVH your God has given you" (a voluntary offering – what you give is to be carefully determined by you)
- Joshua 4 & 5 gives account of the events surrounding, the instructions for, and celebration of the first Passover that

took place in the Promised Land immediately after Israel crossed the Jordan River. *"The people of Israel camped at Gilgal, and they observed Pesach on the fourteenth day of the month, there on the plains of Jericho. The day after Pesach they ate what the land had produced, matzah and roasted ears of the grain that day. The following day, after they had eaten food produced in the land, the manna ended. From that day on the people of Israel no longer had manna; instead, that year, they ate the produce of the land of Kena'an."* – Joshua 5:10-12

The whole House of Isra'el – all twelve tribes- were at that time one nation with YHVH as their King. Over the following centuries the people of Israel wavered back and forth between being devoutly loyal to their Husband King to tragic years of living outside the Torah and worshipping pagan gods. Most of the Old Testament contains record of their successes and failures in their relationship with YHVH. On several occasions, it was only because of His promises to Abraham, Isaac, and Jacob that YHVH did not utterly destroy them. Yes, He loved them despite their inconsistences and unfaithfulness. However, another Kingdom principle was also at work. YHVH is the King of the Universe…and a true and good king never breaks a covenant, promise, or decree. He is eternally bound by His word.

After the reign of Solomon, the great Kingdom of Israel became divided. The southern kingdom became known as the Kingdom of Judah. Its citizens comprised the tribes of Judah, Benjamin, and half of Levi (the priests of YHVH and the caretakers of the Temple). Over time the nations would shorten the name of these peoples from Judah to Jews. These are the people that preserved the Torah and kept the ordinances of YHVH which included his Shabbat and Feast Days. When their kingdom eventually fell and the Temple (both the first in 586 BC and the second in 70 AD) was destroyed, their lands became known as Judea. They were conquered by many kingdoms, but never ceased in their role of preserving and being YHVH's light to the nations. Many of the Kingdom of Judah scattered among the nations, either by force or to pursue a better life, yet they kept their beliefs and practices wherever they went. Others of the nations converted to their faith, which was in keeping with God's design and purpose for them. Often lost in traditions and forgetting the essence of the God they claim to serve, YHVH often refers to them as His unfaithful wife. Yet, today's Jews still preserve the Torah and celebrate His Feast Days. His love for them remains true and their calling is irrevocable because the King cannot break His Word!

But what about the rest of Israel? The northern Kingdom? They were initially called the Kingdom of Israel and were also called the Kingdom of Ephraim, which was the largest tribe in that realm. Their rebellion against the throne in Jerusalem became a complete rebellion against the Throne in Heaven as well. The northern Kingdom of Israel/Ephraim fell to the Assyrians in 722 BC. The Assyrians deported most of these Israelites to locations throughout their empire. The tribes of the northern Kingdom of Israel/Ephraim became the lost tribes, or lost sheep, of Israel, scattered among and absorbed by the nations in which they chose to live. Having previously left the Torah in the dust, they now embraced the pagan gods with abhorrent practices and the godless lifestyles of their host nations and cultures. YHVH grew angry with them. Though He still loved them, Ephraim He did divorce. Though they became lost in the nations, He did not forget their hidden identities a part of the whole House of Israel. Even today, He knows who they are and exactly where they are located! According to Ezekiel, YHVH is determined that the day is coming – in fact, it has arrived – that He will reunite Judah and Ephraim as one stick in His hand. They will become one people again, with one Shepherd and one King. They will be His people and He will dwell with them! (Ezekiel 37). This will be, as Paul said, life from the dead! The dry bones in both camps will have flesh on their bones and become the mighty army of the King of Israel.

Lost Then Found

Throughout Israel's history, there were periods of time that Passover was lost - along with many other elements of the culture, system, and faith that YHVH had called them to. But there was always a remnant that preserved what YHVH had given...and always a Godly leader who would bring them back to the Ways of the King.

- II Chronicles 29 – 31 King Hezekiah's reign over the southern Kingdom of Judah was Godly. He very quickly had Solomon's Temple purified and fully restored the worship of YHVH in the Holy Place. He also succeeded in calling the people of both the Southern and Northern Kingdoms – Judah and Israel (Ephraim) – to come to Jerusalem for the Second Passover. (The Temple and priesthood were not ready for the Passover of the first month.) Re-establishing and leading the nation in God's Ways, Hezekiah prosperously ruled over the Kingdom of Judah for 29 years.

- II Chronicles 35 and 2 Kings 22 – 23:30 King Josiah, while ruling over the southern Kingdom of Judah, destroyed all the pagan items and practices of Ba'al and Ishtar worship that had been assimilated into the people and land of Judah. He returned the kingdom to the Torah and re-established the observance of Passover. King Josiah was the last righteous king over Judah before YHVH caused it to begin to collapse. Josiah was killed in battle against Egypt in Megiddo. His son, Jehoiakim, ruled Judah for eleven years under submission to Egypt. He turned the kingdom away from YHVH again. In 586 BC, Having already defeated the Assyrians and thus gaining what once was the Northern Kingdom of Israel, Babylon invaded and took control over Judah, the Jews. Thus began the 70 years of Babylonian captivity.

- Ezra 6:19-22 Though King Cyrus of Persia (conquerors over Babylon) had allowed the Judeans (Jews) to return and rebuild the walls and city of Jerusalem, it was under the reign of his son, Darius I, that they were able to rebuild the Temple. Ezra records, *"The people from the exile kept Pesach (Passover) on the fourteenth day of the first month. ... The people of Isra'el who had returned from exile and all those who had renounced the filthy practices of the nations living in the land in order to seek YHVH the God of Isra'el, ate the Pesach lamb and joyfully kept the Feast of Matzah (Unleavened Bread) for seven days."* (Ezra 6:19,21-22)

The Jews remained able to keep Jerusalem, their Temple with the worship of YHVH, and the observance of His Shabbats and Feast Days intact until the Seleucid Greek reign of Antiochus Epiphanes as he crushed Jerusalem in 169 BC. At that time, Antiochus destroyed the city, turned the Temple over to the worship of Zeus, outlawed the Torah, and forbade its instruction and observance. This continued until Antiochus was defeated in 165 BC by Judas Maccabee, his four brothers, and their followers. This important restoration of the Torah, the Temple, the Torah lifestyle, and the observance of Shabbats and YHVH's Feast Days is still celebrated today. The celebration is called Hanukkah – the Feast of Dedication.

Where does Yeshua fit in this history of two kingdoms? Scripture makes it quite clear that He is of the direct lineage of King David and King Solomon. He has fulfilled and is all that the ancient prophets of Israel foresaw. His is and always will be the Lion of Judah, the rightful King of Israel...the Whole House/Kingdom of Israel. He is indeed Jewish – of the tribe of Judah – and always will be. He is the one who will bring the entire Kingdom of Israel back together again. He revealed with his own words that this was a part of His calling. He came to seek and save that which was lost. He came for the lost sheep of Israel. He came to bring that prodigal son, Ephraim, home again. He reunites them with those of their older brother, Judah, who also recognize and embrace Him as their Messiah and King. Yeshua came so *all* who are of His Bride, Israel, would become clean, pure, beautiful, and prepared for Him! Yeshua (who is YHVH in the flesh) and His Bride pledged themselves to each other at Mount Sinai. The Wedding Covenant agreed upon on that Day of Betrothal will be kept. When the Father sees that the Bride is restored and has made herself ready, the Groom will come for her!

Has Messiah called you to himself? Have you heard the Shepherd's voice beckoning you home? Have you returned? Are you restored to being His Bride once again? Most likely you are of one of those two kingdoms, friend. You are of Judah and have recognized Him as Messiah. (Even some of Judah got lost in the nations - hiding in Christianity to save their lives, then discovering their Messiah. My family is of that lot.) Or you are of Ephraim, once a lost sheep of Israel dispersed in the nations, ignorant of your true identity. But now you are home with Him in His Kingdom where you belong.

(Keep in mind, only a portion of Israel is Caucasian. New studies are identifying direct descendants among African tribes, Native American tribes, in India, and in China!) The King is restoring His House, His Kingdom. Those outside of the descendants of Abraham are welcomed with open arms. YHVH has always kept the door of His Kingdom open to foreigners so that they too become citizens of Israel fully able to experience His goodness and receive His inheritance. Great days of restoration for the entire earth are ahead. The King is about to deliver His People once again by his mighty, outstretched hand! We have His Covenant Promise on that!

Welcome to what Passover is all about!

Chapter Three:
Yeshua's Passover

Passover is a Never-Ending Celebration

Sadly, most of the Christian church has left the observance of Passover. This loss goes back to the days of the Roman Empire and the successful efforts of Emperor Constantine in the early 4th century BCE to unite his military and his empire. Rome had become deeply divided between those of Roman paganism and an increasing number of Christians. Though remaining a lifetime worshipper of the sun god, Mithras, Constantine claimed to be a convert to the Christian faith. He then declared himself to be the head of the Roman church and selected his own council of church leaders. He now held a dual headship over both the pagan and Christian religions which would allow the two worlds to co-exist within his empire.

However, Rome's hatred of Judea and the Jews remained a deeply imbedded issue and Constantine determined to strip anything Jewish from his new version of the Christian church. Observance of the seventh-day Sabbath (Shabbat) was forbidden as a Christian practice, and the Feast Days were abolished. What Constantine, his council, and the numerous councils of the Roman church decreed over the next decades and the following several centuries forever changed what had been the faithful, Torah-based walk of those who had chosen to follow the Hebrew and very Jewish Messiah of the first century. Threatened with death and told that if they refused to change their ways they would be eternally separated from Christ, many Christians unwittingly adapted to the decrees of Roman church. Groups of believers like the Waldensians had already moved into Alps of central Europe as early as 300 AD to preserve the seventh-day Sabbath and the study of the Old Testament. Similar groups had already formed elsewhere, such as the Celtic Church of Ireland. Such groups considered themselves to be Apostolic churches, planted by 1st and 2nd century missionaries. Their remote locations became a protection against Roman Catholicism for many years. For over 1400 years the edicts of the Roman Church and its Popes resulted in the imprisonment and death of Jews and Torah-based Christians by the millions.

What bearing does Constantine's actions have on what exists in today's Christian churches? The ugly truth is that the church (meaning us) has become guilty of the same issues of abandoning YHVH that has plagued Israel since the time of Moses. Not unlike our Hebrew ancestors, in looking to appease and blend in with the cultures in which they found themselves living, many church forefathers bowed to Constantine and the ongoing demands of the Roman Church - and many unknowingly still do so today. Without being aware, we continue to blindly obey the decrees of a human emperor over the decrees of the One we claim to be the King of kings and the only King to whom we will bow. Sadly, a dark deception is still in place.

History tells us that Constantine moved YHVH's Holy Days to match those of the pagan gods Rome worshipped. Jews and Christians were forbidden to worship their God on the seventh-day Sabbath. If they wanted to worship their God, YHVH, they must do so on the venerable Day of Sun God, the Lord's Day of Sunday. Then Constantine and his Councils addressed the birth of IESVS/Jesu/Jesus (no longer could He called by his Hebrew name, Yeshua). Though Jews and early Christians did not celebrate a person's birthday, in the Roman culture birthdays were important. Constantine worshipped the sun god Mithras. Though most followers of Yeshua recognized that Scripture gives strong indication that Messiah's birth took place during the Fall Feast season, Constantine appointed December 25th, the birthday of the son (Tammuz) of the sun god (Mithras/Nimrod), to be honored as the birthday of the Son of the Christian God. The celebration of the winter solstice, another element of the worship of the sun god, spanned over several days as the Feast of Saturnalia. Both pagan celebrations were intertwined with the elements of the account of Christ's birth and became known under Constantine's Roman Church as Christmas. Up until the 1880's, Christmas remained so pagan and raucous in its festivities that most Christians refused to participate. In fact, in the U.S.A. the holiday of Christmas was not observed in most states until 1870. Nonetheless, the pagan Romans and the Christian Romans would now forever be unified in a time of winter celebration that had nothing to do with Israel's Messiah.

Constantine did the same with Passover. On the Roman calendar, Passover always fell near the pagan feast day honoring the goddess Ishtar (Astarte/Semiramis). Ishtar was the mother of Tammuz, the son of the sun god Mithras. This springtime celebration honored the rebirth of life on earth and the pagan belief in the resurrection of Tammuz, who had been killed by a boar (thus the Romans ate ham in his honor). Ishtar was to have arrived on earth inside an egg (she is the fertility goddess) and her animal companions were rabbits, known for their reproductive ability. Constantine conveniently moved the celebration of the death and resurrection of Jesus, the Son of God, to coincide with the Feast of Ishtar. The Latin name for this goddess is Ostrea, from which we get its English form, Easter. By separating the death and resurrection of Yeshua from

Passover, Constantine and the Roman Church's on-going Councils hoped to further strip the Jewishness of being a Christian from the Church. They succeeded.

The great tragedy that resulted in mixing Roman paganism with the Torah-based celebrations of the Kingdom of YHVH is the horrible anti-Semitic hatred of anything Jewish or of Israel that eventually permeated much of Christianity. False doctrines such as Replacement Theology (the belief that the Church has replaced Israel as God's chosen people) has fed this hatred, thus mentally and spiritually rebuilding the Wall of Separation between Jew and Gentile that Yeshua died to destroy. The Great Reformation and the birth of Protestantism (protesting Roman Catholics) failed to address this heresy. Regrettably, Martin Luther was well known for his hatred of Jews and called for the death of Jews and the destruction of their synagogues.

YHVH's Feast Days and Sabbath, which He decreed were to be perpetual (meaning *never-ending*), became designated throughout Christendom as too Jewish for Christians, who claim to be loving and loyal to the Jewish Messiah. Is it only me, or does something not add up in this equation?

Today, many Christians are waking up. This is indeed the mighty, outstretched hand of YHVH at work! The King decreed that Jew and Gentile would become one stick in His hand before Messiah would be able to return. No more Kingdom of Judah. No more Kingdom of Ephraim. Only Isra'el. One Kingdom with one King. One Flock with One Shepherd. One Bride with the one and only Groom. One Nation who would be His People and with whom He will dwell. The King cannot and will not break His word! In our time, Christians are beginning to abandon the Lord's Day of Sunday and return to the biblical Sabbath (Shabbat) established by YHVH our God and observed by Yeshua and the Apostles. These Christians are questioning the trappings of Christmas and starting to celebrate the Feast of Tabernacles. The bunnies, eggs, and pagan nonsense of Easter is fading away in the homes of many believers. They are recognizing how important the observance of Passover is in fully understanding Messiah's death and resurrection. A remnant amongst these Christians has completely crossed back over to the Hebrew roots of the faith and left the still very Romanized church entirely. They observe the seventh-day Sabbath and the Feast Days according to YHVH's instruction and Yeshua's teachings. Make no mistake, Yeshua is their Messiah and their salvation is fully based on God's grace provided fully and only in Him. They have returned to the whole House of Israel, just as Ezekiel prophesied. Their number is growing.

Yeshua and His Pesach

Contrary to what some theologians teach, Yeshua did not come to earth to start a new religion called Christianity. He did not come to eliminate the Torah, which hold *His* Principles and Instructions for *His* People, and is the very foundation on which *His* Kingdom of earth stands. During Yeshua's life on earth His habit and custom was to be in the synagogue every Shabbat and be in Jerusalem for the Feast Days. In fact, many of the teachings recorded by the apostles in the books of Matthew, Mark, Luke, and John were given by our Messiah in the setting of either a Shabbat or one of the Feast Days. Even though He knew quite well that His followers would one day be kicked out of the synagogues because they carried His teachings and bore testimony of His resurrection, His heart's intent was to help both Jew and Gentile return to the grace-filled, freedom-giving purity of the Torah (God's Ways). In short, all His teachings, and His death and resurrection, served one purpose: to bring both wandering sides of His Bride back into the Kingdom of YHVH so that we could learn how to live as blessed children in the Father's House of Israel again. He knows that He cannot return and reign with us on earth until this happens. The Bride of Israel's King must be of Israel.

With this understanding, it is time to look with open eyes at the role of Pesach (Passover) in the earthly life of our Messiah. In the New Testament, the following Scriptures tell of his connection to Pesach as a part of His very Jewish lifestyle.

Luke 2:41-49   Yeshua, at age 12, travels to Jerusalem with his family for Pesach and remains behind to "be about his Father's business". This takes place at the time a Jewish boy reaches manhood; thus he was responsible to YHVH's instruction that every man of Israel come before YHVH on Pesach. Yeshua was also the firstborn son of his earthly parent's household and the firstborn son of God. To fulfill YHVH's instructions regarding the firstborn at Pesach, his participation was essential. When his parents left Jerusalem in one of the caravans heading back to Galilee, Yeshua stayed behind in the Temple, causing a frantic search by Joseph and Mary. He was found in the Temple courts among the rabbis, listening, questioning, and astonishing them with his insights and wisdom. When confronted by his parents, he said to them. *"Why do you have to look for me? Didn't you know that I had to be concerning myself with my Father's affairs?"*

John 2:13-25   Yeshua's first cleansing of the Temple took place during the time of Pesach. *"He made a whip from cords and drove them all out of the Temple grounds, the sheep and cattle as well. He knocked over the money-changers' tables, scattering their coins; and to the pigeon-sellers he said, 'Get these things out of here! How dare you turn my Father's house into a market!'"* Once again, He is in the Temple grounds, concerning His Father's affairs. Also, on this occasion, He proclaimed concerning himself, *"Destroy this temple, and in three days I will raise it up again."* This would take place in during another Passover week not too far in His future. (Yeshua cleansed the Temple a second time, again during the Passover season, proclaiming *"The Tanakh (Old Testament) says, 'My house is to be a house of prayer,' but you have made it into a den of robbers!"* Luke 19:45-48)

John 6:1-71   So much is packed into this chapter, all taking place as Pesach was approaching. The feeding of the five thousand, the calming of the Sea of Galilee during a storm on an overnight boat trip to Capernaum, and the turning back of disciples who could not accept His deeper teaching concerning His flesh and blood. In these passages, the foundation of eternal life that would be established by His Passover death and resurrection was laid out in His teachings. He identified himself as the living manna, the Bread of Life come down from heaven so that we could live forever. He made it clear that this bread - His own flesh - and His blood would be essential for eternal deliverance from the curse of sin, which is death. He spoke of the power that is His to raise up on the Last Day those who believe in Him and live their lives as He does. They were words spoken in the Spirit who gives life, yet many could not understand or trust. He declared, *"No man can come to me unless the Father has made it possible for him."* He asked the Twelve if they too were going to leave him, to which Peter replied, *"Lord, to whom would we go? You have the word of eternal life. We have trusted, and we know that you are the Holy One of God."*

John 11:55-12:49

Once again the time for Pesach was approaching. Jews were starting to flock to Jerusalem to prepare and to cleanse themselves in the pools surrounding the Temple grounds. Many were looking for Yeshua, but He had not yet arrived. Six days before Pesach He came to Beit-Anyah (Bethany) to the home of Lazarus and his sisters. A special dinner was prepared in His honor. During the meal Miryam (Mary) washed and anointed Yeshua's feet with expensive oil, an act for which she was severely criticized by all except Him. Crowds from Jerusalem heard He was there and began to arrive to see Him – and to see Lazarus who He had previously raised from the dead. Yeshua's triumphal entry into Jerusalem then took place, and what transpired over the next days and weeks changed the world.

Matthew 26-28 Matthew's account of the Pesach death and resurrection of Yeshua

Mark 14-16 Mark's account of the Pesach death and resurrection of Yeshua

Luke 22-24 Luke's account of the Pesach death and resurrection of Yeshua

John 13-20:24 John's account of the Pesach death and resurrection of Yeshua

Yeshua's Last Pesach on Earth

We are now ready to look at Pesach as Yeshua experienced it during the final hours before His crucifixion. Simply by seeing and understanding the exact timing of the King of the Universe in the events in the life of His Son during the Season of Our Liberation, we can begin to grasp 1) the depth of the meaning of Yeshua's sacrifice in relation to YHVH's eternal covenant with His people, Israel and 2) how all the Feast Days of the King serve to prophetically spell out YHVH's plan of redemption for humankind and all His creation. As you discover the intricate details of YHVH's hand in the unfolding of this ancient event in Messiah's life, you will soon agree that we love and serve an absolutely amazing God.

A quick review is in order. We must keep in mind that the observance of Pesach is in YHVH's written covenant with Israel. God cut a foundational covenant with Abraham, promising that his descendants would be as many as the stars in the sky, and promising to give to them a land that would stretch from Egypt to the Euphrates River. (Genesis 15). With the deliverance of the Hebrews from Egypt, YHVH took the Hebrew people, now numbering at least over a million strong, to Mount Sinai and there gave them a written agreement and recorded history called the Torah in which He pledges to care for and prosper them. In return, Israel pledges to live according to the agreement and follow YHVH as their one God forever. This is literally an exchange of vows, so much so that God, in His own words recorded by the prophets who followed, constantly refers to Israel as His wife...His betrothed bride. It is with His bride, Israel, that He longs to dwell forever. The King of the Universe has chosen His eternal bride, and to this sealed covenant between them He will remain faithful at all costs.

The Feasts of YHVH established in the Torah are far more than simply annual Kingdom celebrations. They are reminders. They remind the Bride of her identity. They give the Bride opportunities to meet face to face with her Groom as she continues to prepare herself, and He continues to prepare a place for her where they can dwell together forever. These important Appointed Times remind the Bride of God's prophetic promises to Israel. They are to be signs to her that their Wedding Day is indeed approaching. As Israel sees each prophetic sign in the Feast Days being fulfilled, she knows where she is to be in her preparations. That is, if she is paying attention. Nothing is being left to chance by her Groom. He has not left out a single detail for her.

Fast forward to Yeshua. With His own Son, Yeshua, Israel's Messiah, YHVH begins to fulfill the marriage covenant. He begins with Pesach, the first of the Covenant's seven Appointed Times between YHVH and His Bride. Pesach indeed provides an annual rich remembrance of Israel's miracle-filled deliverance from Egypt. But it is far more than that. All the imagery and instruction given by YHVH for Pesach also prophetically speaks of His plan of redemption, first for the Jew and then for all mankind. Yeshua also speaks of a great Passover celebration to come when He will drink the cup of Passover with His disciples again. Yes, Passover has a past, a present, and a future. All the King's Feasts do. Passover is just the beginning of His unfolding plan.

Through Yeshua, YHVH begins to fulfill this prophetic promise to His Bride. He does not violate His own prophecy. He is a king. He will not break his word. Looking at the final Passover celebration in the life of Yeshua, we see that God sticks completely to the design He created on that very first Passover. What follows is a breakdown of what took place exactly as YHVH declared it should on every Passover. In bringing His own Lamb into this particular Pesach, He does not miss a beat. He follows His own Word.

Aviv 10   Exodus 12:3-5   The Selection of the Passover Lamb

- The unblemished Passover lamb is to be selected and brought into the household. The Jews call this day *Shabbat HaGadol, The Great Sabbath.* In ancient days it was observed no matter on which day of the week it fell on. (Today it is celebrated on the seventh day Sabbath immediately before Passover.)

- *It was on Aviv 10, Shabbat HaGadol, that Yeshua made His Triumphant Entry into the heart of the household of Israel, Jerusalem.* Scholars of ancient times tell us that it was on this day that the Pesach lambs in their first year that had been born in Bethlehem and watched over by the shepherd priests were carefully driven into the city from the Shepherd Fields. The city was packed with Feast pilgrims of all tribes and nations. Those who had not been able to bring unblemished lambs with them would select from these sheep of Bethlehem. It is believed that Yeshua, the Perfect Lamb of

YHVH, followed this procession of the flock of Pesach lambs into the city, riding upon the colt his Father had provided. The crowds had been waiting for His arrival. They heralded His presence by laying their cloaks (prayer shawls) out on the ground before Him and waving palm branches. They shouted "Hosanna!" (Save us!), "Blessed is the King who is coming in the name of ADONAI!", "Shalom in heaven!", and "Glory in the highest places!". Israel, the Bride, had selected her eternal Pesach Lamb without blemish. In the season when historically the Kings of Israel were selected, they had identified their true King. By YHVH's calendar, everything was happening right on time.

Aviv 10 – 13   Examine the Lamb

- While with the household for four days, the lamb was thoroughly inspected to ensure that it is without blemish. An emotional attachment to this innocent creature usually took place during this short period. The giving up of the lamb will be personal. The sacrifice would carry a soul-felt price.

- *After His Triumphant Entry, Yeshua endured four days of intense examination by His disciples, the Pharisees, the Sadducees, and the Sanhedrin. The Lamb was even examined by the Romans (Gentiles) through Herod and Pilate. He was found without fault - without blemish. He was so perfect in His observance of the Torah, His teachings, and in His Godly character that those among the religious Jewish leadership who sought to destroy Him had to present false witnesses to testify against Him. His accusers main charge was that He claimed to be the King of the Jews, the Messiah and Son of God – which in truth, He was and still is.*

Aviv 14   The Night of Passover

- In the time of Yeshua, a difference in understanding and practice existed between the Sadducees and the Pharisees regarding the exact timing for the night of Passover. The Pharisees believed that the dusk hours ending Aviv 13 meant that Aviv 14 was the night of the Passover and the celebration would begin at sunset. The Sadducees believed that the lambs were to be sacrificed by dusk on the day of Aviv 14 with the night of celebration starting at sunset when Aviv 15 would begin. Therefore, the Passover observance in Jerusalem at the time of Yeshua officially began at dusk (about 3 PM) on Aviv 13 with the sacrifice of the lambs and the preparation of the Passover meal by those of the Pharisee persuasion and concluded at sunrise on the morning of Aviv 15, which would be the first day of the Feast of Unleavened Bread (a special Sabbath Day regardless of the day of the week it fell on). The actual sacrifice of the Passover lambs began on Aviv 13 for the Pharisees and ended at 3 PM on Aviv 14 for the Sadducees. The Sadducees at that time oversaw the Temple, thus Jewish religious life, so most of Torah-observant of Israel would have kept the Passover according to the practice of the Sadducees.

- *Follow along closely now!* Here is where YHVH's attention to details - even human details- is remarkable. God's design for his Perfect Lamb be sacrificed at exactly the right time, coupled with Yeshua's intense desire to celebrate the Pesach with His disciples, brought about Messiah's celebration the night before His death. The lamb of their Pesach meal was sacrificed on Aviv 13 and the celebration took place that night beginning Aviv 14. This would satisfy the Pharisees.

But Messiah's last breath of human life would complete the sacrifice of the Prefect Lamb of God at 3 PM on Aviv 14. This would satisfy the Sadducees. The entire 24-hour period of Aviv 14, leading into the Feast of Unleavened Bread was completely covered. There would be no room for human complaint! (Also, keep in mind that the Sadducees did not believe in the resurrection from the dead. Therefore, that Yeshua would align himself with the Pesach observance of the Pharisees should not come as a big surprise.)

- Yeshua's Pesach Seder, which is often called The Last Supper, took place at sunset the evening before His death on Aviv 14. Every account in the Gospel indicates that Yeshua's observance that night was indeed a Passover Seder. Yeshua clearly stated that He had looked forward to celebrating it with His disciples. Every action He made and every word He said that evening would carry a deep meaning that the disciples would not fully understand until after His resurrection. It is not a coincidence that Yeshua commands us to share the unleavened bread of Passover "in remembrance of" Him. Just as lambs were sacrificed and the firstborn of Egypt not spared to purchase the freedom of Israel from Egypt, the Lamb of God who is the firstborn of YHVH purchased with His sacrifice our freedom from bondages created by our own sinfulness. From this night forward we are to remember that both events accomplished what YHVH had destined for us by His mighty and outstretched hand.

Some have asked me if the disciples would have smeared the blood of the lamb of their sacrifice on the doorway (the two sides and the top) that evening. All my studies indicate that this was still the practice in Judea until the destruction of the Second Temple in 70 AD. Thus, I believe that they did. The full tradition of the ancient culture of that time would also have stipulated that some of lamb's blood be poured into a narrow, shallow trough on the threshold. The blood that remained in the bowl would be set in a depression carved into the stone of the threshold. One would have to step under, through, and over the blood to enter a home. Doing so created a threshold covenant of mutual honor and protection with those inside. The deep meaning of this and its implications for us as members of YHVH's household is amazing but must be left for another day and time!

Later in this book you will find a Messianic Passover Seder and a Guide through the Week of Passover crafted for followers of Yeshua. As you read through these, you will discover the incredible significance of every word and action of Messiah in relation to the traditional Passover meal and the detailed events of His death and resurrection. On that night of Passover, the disciples knew the celebration routine since their childhoods. They knew the story of the Exodus by heart in every detail. They thought they knew what to expect. However, as Yeshua unfolded for them its deeper prophetic meaning regarding himself, He gave them images of who He is that would affect their service to Him and others the rest of their lives. Though they did not fully understand until much later, it was impossible to miss God's redemptive plan unfolding through Messiah that evening. YHVH had designed this plan with Him before the foundations of the earth. Moses and the Exodus were the setup, ensuring that the right people would be in the right place at the right time, for the right reasons. Now Yeshua was about to fulfill every eternal purpose and meaning of this God-ordained time in His universe. It is nothing less than stunning.

For now, hold on to two important insights from Passover and its God-appointed meal. They bear great significance in understanding what some might consider puzzling events of the next day.

- By YHVH's instruction, the Pesach meal must include maror (bitter herbs such as horseradish) and matzah (unleavened bread). The herbs are to remind us of the bitterness of our bondage in slavery to the oppressor. The matzah is to remind us of the hurriedness in which the Israelites left their bondage. Their deliverance took place suddenly and miraculously. Matzah is called "the bread of affliction". The baking process of unleavened bread leaves stripes and piercings that remind the Israelites of the physical harshness of their slavery. The maror would now serve to remind us of the bitterness of our bondage to our oppressor, Satan. The piercing and the stripes of the matzah will forever remind us of the striped and pierced body of Yeshua. As Yeshua broke the matzah at His Pesach Seder, He said to the disciples, *"This is my body, which is being given for you; do this in remembrance of me."* (Luke 22:19) By the next morning they would witness the painful reality of His words.

- According to YHVH's instruction no bones of the Pesach lamb were to be broken, the lamb must be eaten hurriedly, and it had to be fully consumed before sunrise. Nothing was to be left by morning. Though it was the standard Roman crucifixion practice to break the leg bones of the person being crucified, the bones of Yeshua, YHVH's Pesach Lamb, were not broken. His body was removed hurriedly from the cross so that it would not remain until morning. At burial, Yeshua's body was fully consumed by the tomb.

Aviv 14   The Day the Lamb of God Gave Up His Life

Following their Pesach Meal of Remembrance, Yeshua and His disciples crossed the narrow Kidron Valley to the stony base of the Mount of Olives where the Garden of Gethsemane is located. The Garden is an olive grove, complete with wine presses. The location bears that name because in its Hebrew origin Gethsemane means *the place of pressing oils.* As He prayed, Yeshua was hard-pressed by what He knew lie ahead of him. Sweat poured from His brow like blood. The struggle was intense. His heart was being examined by the Father of our Household. Would the Lamb remain pure and determined to fulfill His destiny, keeping His focus on the joy of what His sacrifice would bring to the Kingdom? Would He remain in submission to the King of the Universe, the Father, with whom He was one? The Lamb was under the Father's final examination.

Even in His arrest and trials, the Lamb remained without anger, without any action or word in violation of his Father's Word or will. He stood before the Sanhedrin. He stood before Herod. He stood before Pilate. Some falsely accused him. Herod despised him. Pilate knew he was innocent. His examination as the Pesach Lamb of YHVH was complete.

The Perfect Lamb was spat on, beaten, flogged, and His beard torn from his face. He was stripped down in shame, wore a robe of mockery, and bore a crown of thorns thrust on His head that tore His flesh and caused blood to run into His eyes and down His face. To those who knew him He was almost unrecognizable. Yet He remained without anger, without any action or word in violation of His Father's Word or will. No man would take His life. He would give it up willingly. The eternal purpose was too great. He had known this day was coming since before the earth was formed. He would see it through. This Passover would be unlike any other before. There would be none other like it again.

The religious leaders of the Sanhedrin were becoming frantic. By their ruling, the great Passover of all Israel was only hours away. If this man were to die it needed to happen immediately, before dusk arrived. The timing, they thought, would serve them. Everyone would be too busy with their sacrifices and preparations. Yet that was not the case. The entire city was becoming aware of what was going on. Crowds were forming. Yeshua had stirred the hearts of too many. Too many had seen the miracles and heard Him teach. Those who had believed in Him were crushed to numbness. Others wanted to see what the Man of God would do. Would He be able to save himself? Would God intervene in some mighty, miraculous way? The hatred of Rome was stirred up too. Herod and Pilate were trapped on every side. Pilate tried to create a human means of escape for Yeshua…but his good intentions backfired. The Lamb would be sacrificed. Another Passover deliverance, of greater proportion and meaning than the first, would take place.

We know that the lambs of YHVH's Pesach were to be sacrificed at dusk so that all could be in their homes between sunset and complete darkness for the beginning of the Night of Nights. Over the centuries before this greatest of Passovers, the religious leaders of Israel came to interpret "dusk" to be between three in the afternoon and sunset. Every priest in Israel was on assignment in the Temple to assist with and carry out the sacrifices. As the heads of the households of Israel waited in lines at the temple for the body of their lamb to be returned to them, others of their households scurried about putting all else in place and prepared the fires that would roast the most important element of their meal. But this Passover was odd. The streets were unrestful. There were stories and rumors racing like a wildfire. Soldiers were everywhere, on alert for outbreaks of rebellion. All were uneasy and their faces bore traces of confusion and uncertainty. Then, at noon the sky went dark. The sun disappeared behind fierce dark clouds.

In the Temple, the Passover sacrifices that began the day before continued amid the growing concern. The last of the Passover lambs was sacrificed at 3:00 PM on Aviv 14. When that last sacrifice was complete the High Priest raised his bloodstained hands and declared to Israel, "It is finished!" The Gospel accounts tell us that at that precisely 3:00 PM Yeshua cried out with his dying breath, "It is finished!" (Luke 23:44-46) The earth shook. Huge boulders split apart. The Temple priests were thrown into terror-filled panic when, like when a Hebrew father who tears his prayer shawl down its center when a son dies, the parokhet (the curtain in the Temple that separated the Holy of Holies from all else) ripped in two. There was nothing quiet or ordinary about this Passover. The city was thrown into turmoil and confusion.

There must have been a certain Spirit-given calmness amongst some who had followed Yeshua. Somehow, amid the commotion and their own deep shock and sorrow, they kept their focus on following Messiah's instruction. "If you love Me, keep My commandments." It was now dusk. The Night of Nights and the High Sabbath it ushers into the world were but a few short hours away. This would be a day of complete rest. No work is to be done. The day would be a High Sabbath as it fell on a day other than a regular Sabbath. YHVH had instructed them not to touch a dead body on Passover. He had told them not to bury the dead on any Sabbath...especially on a High Sabbath. They love Him. If they were to keep His instruction they must work quickly.

One of the faithful, a wealthy man named Joseph, approached Pilate and asked for Yeshua's body to be given to him. Joseph took the body, wrapped it in a clean linen sheet, and laid it in the tomb he had been preparing for his own use someday. It was cut out of rock with a large stone set to roll in front its entrance. The body was placed inside. The stone was rolled into place. Mary of Magdala and another Mary witnessed the burial, heartbroken that there had not been any time to properly anoint and prepare the body according to the customs of their people. They would return when both Sabbaths – the High Sabbath of Passover and the regular Sabbath that would follow it – were complete. They called that day Yom Rishon, First Day. The Romans called it Sunday…the Day of the Sun God. When the markets reopened after sunset at the end regular Sabbath (the day called Saturn's Day by the Romans), they would go out to buy the needed oils and spices. First thing in the morning on Yom Rishon they would properly care for Messiahs' body.

Aviv 15   The Passover Sabbath and the First day of the Feast of Unleavened Bread

The next day, as Israel observed the High Sabbath following the night of Passover, the priests and the Pharisees approached Pilate and begged him to set a guard in place to secure the tomb. These leaders believed in the resurrection of the dead and they did not want any trickery going on to give the appearance that Yeshua had come back to life. Pilate concurred and the stone was sealed in place. Guards were stationed. On this Passover Sabbath on a Sixth Day (Friday) all seemed peaceful and under control. Another Sabbath was soon to begin. Though a search was on for Peter, James, John, and for the rest of the remaining eleven core group of Yeshua's follower's things seemed to be slowly calming down. How tragic it was to learn of the suicide of Judas, whom the Chief Priest had paid to betray his Rabbi.

To prevent any confusion in this narrative, it is important to know that in the year of Yeshua's death the High Sabbath of Passover was back-to-back with the regular Sabbath. This means that Yeshua died on a Thursday afternoon, Aviv 14, at 3:00 PM and was placed in the tomb before the start of the night of Pesach at sunset. That sunset ushered in the High Sabbath of Passover, which fell on a Friday (Sixth Day), Aviv 15. The next day, Aviv 16, was in that year a regular Sabbath. This means that for two days the women who followed Him were unable to attend to His body.

The Gospel accounts tell us that the women went early, before sunrise, to the tomb hoping to gain access to his body. When they arrived, He was already gone. This means that Yeshua rose from the dead sometime before this. Remember, the Hebrew day starts with nightfall. The first day of the week, Yom Rishon (Sunday for the Romans) had already begun the evening before. We can now do the math from a Hebrew perspective! Yeshua died at dusk on Aviv 14 and was placed in the tomb that evening, Aviv 15, by Joseph. Aviv 15 and 16 passed by as *both* were Sabbaths that year. The Feast of Matzah was now fully underway. Sometime between evening and sunrise on Aviv 17 Yeshua came back to life! This also means that Yeshua's bodwas lifeless for a full 3 days before He was resurrected. (half day on Aviv 14, full day on Aviv 15, full day on Aviv 16, half day on Aviv 17 = 3 days)

The timing of YHVH is amazing. Give this some thought for a moment. Yeshua had to be born in a specific year to allow for the Passover High Sabbath and the regular Sabbath to fall back-to-back in the year of His death. This allowed for a full three days to transpire from the night of Passover to the day eternally assigned to be His Resurrection Day. What day was that? **The Day of First Fruits!!!** As Paul tells us with absolute certainty, and fully based upon the timing of the King of the Universe; Yeshua is the First Fruit of the Resurrection!

In the Gospel of Matthew this becomes quite apparent!

> *But Yeshua, again crying out in a loud voice, yielded up his spirit. At that moment the parokhet in the Temple was ripped in two from top to bottom; and there was an earthquake, with rocks splitting apart. Also the graves were opened, and the bodies of many holy people who had died were raised to life; and after Yeshua rose, they came out of the graves and went into the holy city, where many people saw them.* **Matthew 27: 50-53**

The parallels between the observance of Passover, The Feast of Unleavened Bread, and the Day of First Fruits as given to Israel by YHVH in the Torah and the events of Yeshua's Passover meal with the disciples, His trials and crucifixion, and His resurrection are striking and certainly not by coincidence. We can readily see that Passover and its attached Feast Days was an ordained time on YHVH's calendar that was designed for specific and on-going redemptive purpose. Passover, the Feast of Unleavened Bread, and the Day of Fruits celebrate liberation from bondage and redemption from death. In a remarkable way, this 3-to-4-day period became a great supernatural, Covenant-based exchange. The people of Israel (the Bride) brought to YHVH their Pesach sacrifice and First Fruit offerings…and in exchange, YHVH (the Groom) brought His. Our betrothal has come at a high price, sealed by shed blood provided by both parties. God's determination to save, purify, redeem, and preserve those who are his Bride goes beyond human reasoning. It is nothing less than a stunning testimony of the nature of YHVH and His love for us.

Hopefully by this point, you have come to an understanding that to separate the observance and celebration of our Messiah's death and resurrection from the context of the observance of Passover is a sad error. This is true for two reasons. First, outside of the proper context how can we possibly grasp the depth of what was being accomplished by Yeshua on that particular Pesach? There are layers of truth and meaning that we will not even begin to touch on in this book. In fact, in every observance year by year, I learn more and see more. I am sure it will take eternity for me to grasp all there is to be found in Passover in regard to our Messiah!

Second, we should not be surprised that Jews around the globe cannot accept a faith in Yeshua their Messiah when the church has so far removed Him from what Israel already knows of God's Truth. They cannot and never will abandon Passover as it was eternally established by God for His people. Until we put Yeshua's death and resurrection back into Passover and place His entire earthly life and teachings back into the context of His people, they cannot even begin to recognize Him. To them, our Greco Roman/European/American Jesus just does not measure up. At best, some will consider Him a wonderful rabbi, maybe even a prophet. But Messiah? No. Messiah will not abandon YHVH's Ways. Easter? Christmas? Absolutely not. They are not able to give Him a serious look.

Until Ephraim (the lost sheep in the world, now a part of the Gentiles) and Judah (the Jews) can embrace Messiah Yeshua as the King of one Israel, the Shepherd over one flock, He will not be able to return for us. He will not have a divided, confused, and unprepared Bride. That may sound harsh to some, but it is truth. To truly honor Him and the destiny He has irrevocably called us to, we must return to His Ways. He died to make eternal forgiveness and the ability to return fully possible. We must love and embrace both the King *and* His Kingdom's Ways. It is time to for both Jew and Gentile to come home to live in the Father's House once again abundantly.

I can think of no better time than the King's Passover to be reunited in Him!

Chapter Four:
Passover in the Apostles and Prophets

The Apostles and Pesach

In the early church, the observance of Pesach (Passover) never stopped. Rather, Pesach had now become more important than ever before! Imagine for a moment the powerful and moving memories (remembrances) each Pesach brought to the forefront in the hearts and minds of those who had witnessed first-hand the Passover death, burial and resurrection of Messiah? Imagine being one of the living eleven who had sat at the table the night of Messiah's last Pesach meal on earth? Imagine what this all meant to those who had seen Him on the road to Emmaus, in their hiding places where He appeared to them, and in the Galilee. Those forty days had to be mind-blowing!

To think that these through whom the Good News of the Kingdom would be established around the world would abandon Passover does not make any sense at all. They most certainly did not. They did not leave the faith of Abraham, Isaac, and Jacob. They honored the Sabbath and the Feast Days just as they had witnessed Yeshua do. They confessed him as the Messiah promised to Israel, the son of their God, YHVH. They did as all other devout teachers and prophets of God's Word, including Yeshua, had always done. They called YHVH's people back to the Kingdom and welcomed those of any nation to join in also. Sin could be forgiven! Rebellion against the Creator could be reversed! For those who wanted to enter in, the penalty was gone.

Death had lost its sting! The curse could be lifted for those who love Him and return! The weight the religious leaders had made of YHVH's Word had been lifted. The Torah once again was YHVH's Perfect Law of Freedom!

These passionate first of Yeshua's followers and those who joined them as the Good News spread were eventually ejected from synagogues. Did this stop them? No. They met in homes each Sabbath. They adhered to the Kingdom Ways that Yeshua had refreshed and restored in them. People in Ephesus, with a tone of degradation in their voices, called them "those Christ-followers" …Christians. The term was not meant to be a compliment by either Gentile or Jew. Rome hated them with the same fervor they had in their hatred of Jews.

In their eyes there wasn't any real difference, other than this Messiah that Christians worshipped and followed. For most Gentiles, Christians were considered just another sect in Judaism. Both Jews and these Christians would not bow to the Emperor as a god, or worship any of Rome's hundreds of gods. Both were to be despised.

When we look at the New Testament writings there are not a great number of references that give a "thou shalt" to the Sabbath or the Feast Days. In the minds of those who wrote the gospel accounts and the letters that we now call books, such observances were understood to be a natural part of the lifestyle of any who love and follow the Messiah. We have already established His consistent observance of the seventh-day Sabbath and the Feast Days. His deep attachment to Passover should now be well understood. Now we will examine Passover's place in the writings of the apostles.

Acts 12

The events that take place in this chapter occur during Pesach and the Feast of Unleavened Bread. These things happened several years after Yeshua's death and resurrection. Paul and Barnabas were busy with their work among the Gentiles. Peter had already witnessed and participated in the conversion of Cornelius and his household. Herod Agrippa I had begun arresting and persecuting certain members of what we shall call the Messianic community. He had Jacob (James), John's brother, killed by the sword. Then he sought after Peter, planning to do the same.

> *It was during the Days of Matzah, so when Herod seized him (Kefa/Peter), he threw him in prison, handing him over to be guarded by four squads of four soldiers each, with the intention of bringing him to public trial after Pesach. So Kefa (Peter) was being held under watch in prison, but intense prayer was being made to God on his behalf by the Messianic community.* Acts 12:3-5

The account continues concerning an angel of YHVH that appeared to Peter in prison and made a way of escape for him by opening the iron gates. Peter made his way to the home of Miryam (Mary), the mother of Mark, where many believers had gathered to pray for him. The servant who answered the door was in such shock to see him that she closed the door in his face! No one believed her. Peter kept knocking and eventually they opened the door and rejoiced in his testimony. For their protection he did not stay, certain that Herod's men would soon be on the chase.

I find something fascinating in this account. Luke, the author of the Book of the Acts of the Apostles, made sure the reader, Theophilos, knew the time and season of these events. Why? Because Herod, who had played a huge role in the death of Yeshua during the

Passover a few years earlier, was going to see to it that Peter would also die in the same season! The connection to Passover remained a crucial point to the apostles.

Acts 20

Luke, in his account to Theophilos of his travels with Paul, uses Passover week (the Feast of Unleavened Bread) to identify the time and season of their journey. He also mentions that they were hoping to return to Jerusalem in time to celebrate Shavu'ot...Pentecost. The Feast Days were indeed still being honored and kept!

> *As he (Sha'ul/Paul) was preparing to set sail for Syria, he discovered a plot against him by the unbelieving Jews; so he changed his mind and decided to return by way of Macedonia. Sopater from Berea, the son of Pyrrhus, accompanied him; as did Aristarchus and Secundus from Thessalonica, Gaius from Derbe, Timothy, and Tychicus and Trophimus from the province of Asia. These men went on and waited for us in Troas, while we sailed from Philippi after the Days of Matzah. Five days later, we met them in Troas, where we spent a week. ... Sha'ul had decided to bypass Ephesus on his voyage, in order to avoid losing time in the province of Asia, because he was hurrying to get to Yerushalayim, if possible in time to celebrate Shavu'ot.* **Acts 20:3-6,16**

I Corinthians 5:6-8

In his first writing to the believers in Corinth, Paul addresses a sin issue being tolerated within the Messianic community. He is critical of their pride concerning their tolerance and exhorts them to remove the person involved from their fellowship until he repents and is restored to life in Messiah's ways. Paul's exhortation is presented through a well-crafted analogy using the Passover Seder, the removal of leavening in our midst, and a strong reference to the

Messiah's sacrifice as our Pesach Lamb. The congregation in Corinth was comprised of both Jewish and Gentile believers, and Paul obviously expected both to understand exactly what he was saying.

Adapting to the full celebration and understanding of Passover was an integral part of being in unity with Messiah and with one another. Passover is to be celebrated by followers of Messiah in a state of purity and truth.

> *Your boasting is not good. Don't you know the saying, "It takes only a little hametz (yeast) to leaven a whole batch of dough?" Get rid of the old hametz, so that you can be a new batch of dough, because in reality you are unleavened. For our Pesach lamb, the Messiah, has been sacrificed. So let us celebrate the Seder not with leftover hametz, the hametz of wickedness and evil, but with the matzah (unleavened bread) of purity and truth.* **I Corinthians 5:6-8**

Hebrews 11:23-29

The author of Hebrews, who most scholars believe likely to be Paul or Apollos, pens a wonderful discourse in chapter eleven concerning faith or trust. Faith or trust, in the Hebrew mindset, involves hearing and obeying, for without obedience one is not truly trusting. Trust manifests in action. The two must come together to be truly pleasing to God. In verses 23-29, the author writes concerning Moses and the Israelites of the Exodus. He makes it clear that trust (faith) led to their obedience to do as instructed regarding Passover and even in the crossing of the Red Sea. Of such are the great cloud of witnesses who surround us. We are not to forget those who have kept the faith and, by trusting, heard and obeyed. We are to REMEMBER Moses and the Israelites, and to trust YHVH as they did. One of the key functions of Passover is to remember these events.

> By trusting, the parents of Moshe hid him for three months after he was born, because they saw that he was a beautiful child, and they weren't afraid of the king's decree.
>
> By trusting, Moshe, after he had grown up, refused to be called the son of Pharaoh's daughter. He chose being mistreated along with God's people rather than enjoying the passing pleasures of sin. He had come to regard abuse suffered on behalf of the Messiah as greater riches than the treasures of Egypt, for he kept his eyes fixed on the reward.
>
> By trusting, he left Egypt, not fearing the king's anger; he persevered as one who sees the unseen.
>
> By trusting, he obeyed the requirements for the Pesach, including the smearing of the blood, so that the Destroyer of the firstborn would not touch the firstborn of Isra'el.
>
> By trusting, they walked through the Red Sea as through dry land; when the Egyptians tried to do it, the sea swallowed them up. **Hebrews 11:23-29**

Passover and Prophecies Yet Unfilled

As was mentioned in an earlier chapter, each of God's Appointed Times – including Shabbat – hold in his Kingdom a historic past, a present application or fulfillment, and a future place in his redemptive plan. They are perpetual regulations – never ending Kingdom celebrations.

The first Passover overflowed with prophetic images that would see YHVH's fulfillment through Yeshua. As you celebrate the night of Passover, you will discover the richness of prophecy that became intertwined with the traditions of the evening. Until Yeshua's Passover, the death and resurrection of Israel's Messiah were the unseen part of the night. Below are 2 highlights. The rest you will discover as you celebrate!

- The Pesach lamb of Exodus would become God's Pesach Lamb, Yeshua. We would have to cross over, through and under his shed blood to enter the Father's Kingdom. Messiah's blood would prevent the Destroyer from taking our lives. His body would bear the stripes of the bread of our affliction for our healing. His blood would purify us from sin and become the wine that completes our wedding covenant with him. Only by trusting – hearing and doing – do we enter the realm of his provision and protection.

- God's Torah instructions for Pesach foretold of the coming together of Jew and Gentile as one people of God. Foreigners could join in the celebration of Passover (a coming under the protection of the blood of the lamb), but only if they were circumcised. (Exodus 12:48 and Numbers 9:14) This physical act was an outward sign that they had chosen to leave their worldly beliefs and lifestyle behind and fully embrace the covenant of God with the Hebrew people. To observe Pesach, they had to become a part of His Bride. One must cross over from the ways of the world and became an Israelite. Yeshua and the apostles taught that we too must become circumcised, not as in days of old but circumcised in our hearts. We must choose to leave behind ways that are contrary to his. We must cut off our old ways of thinking and living to become like him. When the heart and mind are made new by this circumcision, a person of any nation and ethnic group can become grafted into Israel (God's Kingdom) and celebrate the Passover of Yeshua!

Amid the celebration and remembrance of the Exodus, the Jewish people have never lost the prophetic significance of Passover. They understand that Passover is just as much a part of their future as God's people as it is a part of their past. That truth became a part of the night's celebration. During the night of Pesach, Malachi 3 will be read aloud, and emphasis given to the promise that God will send Elijah to herald Messiah's coming. They understand that Messiah will provide Israel's final, greatest deliverance and salvation. The return of Elijah has been longed for by Israel for centuries. For this reason, at the Passover table an extra goblet, table setting, and chair is put in place for Elijah. At the end of the Seder (order of service) someone, usually a child, is sent to open the front door to welcome Elijah into their home.

"Look! I am sending my messenger to clear the way before me; and the Lord, whom you seek, will suddenly come to his temple. Yes, the messenger of the covenant, in whom you take such delight— look! Here he comes," says YHVH-Tzva'ot. (Yahweh of Heaven's Armies)

But who can endure the day when he comes? Who can stand when he appears? For he will be like a refiner's fire, like the soapmaker's lye. He will sit, testing and purifying the silver; he will purify the sons of Levi, refining them like gold and silver, so that they can bring offerings to YHVH uprightly. Then the offering of Y'hudah and Yerushalayim will be pleasing to YHVH, as it was in the days of old, as in years gone by.

"Then I will approach you for judgment; and I will be quick to witness against sorcerers, adulterers and perjurers; against those who take advantage of wage-earners, widows and orphans; against those who rob the foreigner of his rights and don't fear me," says YHVH-Tzva'ot. ...

"Remember the Torah of Moshe my servant, which I enjoined on him at Horev, laws and rulings for all Isra'el. Look, I will send to you Eliyahu the prophet before the coming of the great and terrible Day of YHVH. He will turn the hearts of the fathers to the children and the hearts of the children to their fathers; otherwise I will come and strike the land with complete destruction."
Malachi 3:1-5, 22-24

In their gospel accounts, Luke and John record the coming and arrival of Yochanan the Immerser (John the Baptist). They wanted to be sure the readers would understand that this prophecy concerning Elijah was fulfilled before the arrival of Yeshua the Messiah. What Israel had longed for every Passover did happen.

All the people were outside, praying, at the time of the incense burning, when there appeared to him an angel of YHVH standing to the right of the incense altar. Z'kharyah was startled and terrified at the sight.

But the angel said to him, "Don't be afraid, Z'kharyah; because your prayer has been heard. Your wife Elisheva will bear you a son, and you are to name him Yochanan. He will be a joy and a delight to you, and many people will rejoice when he is born, for he will be great in the sight of YHVH. He is never to drink wine or other liquor, and he will be filled with the Ruach HaKodesh (Holy Spirit) even from his mother's womb. He will turn many of the people of Isra'el to YHVH their God. He will go out ahead of

YHVH in the spirit and power of Eliyahu (Elijah) to turn the hearts of fathers to their children and the disobedient to the wisdom of the righteous, to make ready for YHVH a people prepared." **Luke 1:10-17**

In Matthew 11 we find Yeshua addressing the crowds concerning Yochanan the Immerser. He distinctly identified John as the herald of Messiah foretold by Isaiah (Isaiah 40:1-3) and Malachi.

As they were leaving, Yeshua began speaking about Yochanan to the crowds: "What did you go out to the desert to see? Reeds swaying in the breeze? No? then what did you go out to see? Someone who was well dressed? Well-dressed people live in kings' palaces. Nu (I challenge you), so why did you go out? To see a prophet! Yes! and I tell you he's much more than a prophet. This is the one about whom the Tanakh (Old Testament) says, 'See, I am sending out my messenger ahead of you; he will prepare your way before you.'

Yes! I tell you that among those born of women there has not arisen anyone greater than Yochanan the Immerser! Yet the one who is least in the Kingdom of Heaven is greater than he! From the time of Yochanan the Immerser until now, the Kingdom of Heaven has been suffering violence; yes, violent ones are trying to snatch it away. For all the prophets and the Torah prophesied until Yochanan. Indeed, if you are willing to accept it, he is Eliyahu (Elijah), whose coming was predicted. If you have ears, then hear!" **Matthew 11:7-15**

As we anticipate Messiah's return for the full salvation of all Israel and our full redemption in Him, are we also to be looking for Elijah? Are we a part of this Passover prophecy? There are two complimentary viewpoints on this matter that indicate yes, we are.

The first is based on the Great Commission and the ministries of the apostles that were driven by this passion. With them, we all function in the same spirit as Elijah. Our message is the same. We are to go among all the nations, proclaiming the Good News of God's Kingdom and the coming of the Messiah. We too have become heralds of His coming. The words foretelling of John the Baptist apply to us as well. *"It was just as had been written in the book of the sayings of the prophet Yesha`yahu (Isaiah), 'The voice of someone crying out: 'In the desert prepare the way for Adonai (Lord, Master)! Make straight paths for him!'"* (Luke 3:4, Isaiah 40:3)

The second is found in Revelation 11. John wrote in his Revelation of Yeshua the Messiah that before His return there will be two witnesses that will come to Jerusalem and prophesy for 1260 days (3 ½ years). They are called the two olive trees and the two menorahs that stand before the Lord of the earth. Until their days are passed, they will be unharmable and fiercely able to destroy their enemies. They will wield great authority, able to do the mighty things Moses did before the Exodus. They will be hated by many and seen as tormentors in their efforts to bring others into God's deliverance. They will be executed, but after 3 ½ days be resurrected and taken into heaven as their enemies watch them. On that day there will be a great earthquake and a tenth of Jerusalem will be destroyed. 7000 people will die in the tragedy.

Most Bible scholars believe that these two witnesses will be Moses and Elijah. Therefore, in Messianic celebrations of YHVH's Pesach, the remembrance and expectation of Elijah to come once again to herald Messiah's arrival remains a part of the celebration.

But what of Yeshua in a future Passover with us? Did He say anything that would indicate we should look forward to such a thing? Yes! Indeed, He did! In His final Seder with His family (the disciples and those who were with Him that evening, most likely including His brothers and His mother) Yeshua tells them, *"I have really wanted so much to celebrate this Seder with you before I die! For I tell you, it is certain that I will not celebrate it again until it is given its full meaning in the Kingdom of God." Then, taking a cup of wine, he made the b'rakhah (blessing) and said, "Take this and share it among yourselves. For I tell you that from now on, I will not drink the 'fruit of the vine' until the Kingdom of God comes."* (Luke 22:15-18) I don't know about you, but no one ever told me about this promise as I was growing up in the church! Yeshua will celebrate the wine-filled cups of Pesach with all of us again.

Yeshua did not stop there. *"Also, taking a piece of matzah (unleavened bread), he made the b'rakhah (blessing), broke it, gave it to them and said, 'This is my body, which is being given for you; do this in memory of me.' He did the same with the cup after the meal, saying, 'This cup is the New Covenant, ratified by my blood, which is being poured out for you.'"* (Luke 11:19-20) Did you see it? He gave us an instruction. *"Do this in memory of me."* Do what? Break the bread and drink the wine of Passover to *remember your deliverance through Me, at this time, in this season.* Yeshua is telling us, "Do not forget that I am your Pesach Lamb! The day will come when we will celebrate and remember together again!"

Because of the church upbringing of many of us, it is difficult for us to imagine or comprehend that the celebration of Passover is eternal. Yet to the Hebrew mind it seems as natural as can be, something to be expected and rejoiced in. Sometimes we need to be reminded that Yeshua is *the Lamb slaughtered before the world was founded.* (Revelation 13:8) The eternal reality of God's Kingdom is beyond our comprehension! We struggle with the Feast Days because we don't understand how much they are a part of who Messiah is. In Colossians 2:11-15 Paul reminds us that we were circumcised in heart by Yeshua, buried with him, and raised from the dead with him – all Passover events. Then in chapter 2 verses 16-17 he says, *"So don't let anyone pass judgment on you in connection with eating and drinking, or in regard to a Jewish festival or Rosh-Hodesh or Shabbat. These are a shadow of things that are coming, but the body is of the Messiah."* To Paul, YHVH's Appointed Times are still a shadow of things yet to come. Their observance belongs to the body of Messiah – and that, my friend, is us!

Passover happened. It is still happening. There is a Passover celebration that is yet to come. We have so much to look forward to! As mentioned in the previous chapter, a great tragedy (an actual heresy) took place when the Roman Emperor Constantine made it law that Passover be replaced with Easter and forbade the observance of YHVH's Shabbat and Feast Days. Who did he think he was, God? Well, yes, he did think that. Every Roman Emperor was both a king and a god...at least that is what they believed. This Jesus, this Christian God, this Jewish Messiah, this Jewish God – they were nothing special...just new gods to be absorbed into the many gods of Rome. Constantine genuinely believed that he had the supreme authority to dictate to Christians how to worship their God and His Son. He believed that he had every right to cut them off from their God (excommunicate) or kill them if they refused to comply. Tired of persecution and fearful for their lives, many Christians complied. The Roman Catholic Church was born, fully separating followers of the Messiah – and the Messiah himself – from the identity of being Israel that YHVH had destined for them. Satan, the father of lies, had succeeded in another Great Deception.

Since that time, Christians have become lost in confusion in a sea of doctrines, theologies, traditions, and denominations. Some of these still carry the anti-Semitism of Rome. We no longer know Yeshua as He was revealed to the world and meant to be known: The Messiah and King of Israel. We have abandoned YHVH's Passover Lamb and the Passover remembrance of Him as He commanded on that very night. We have abandoned the Torah, the Five Books of Moses, in which Moses wrote of Him. I end this chapter with some particularly important verses to contemplate over with our King and Savior. May His Spirit comfort, guide and instruct you.

> *"But I (Yeshua) have a testimony that is greater than Yochanan's (John's). For the things the Father has given me to do, the very things I am doing now, testify on my behalf that the Father has sent me. In addition, the Father who sent me has himself testified on my behalf. But you have never heard his voice or seen his shape; his word does not stay in you, because you don't trust the one he sent.*

> *You keep examining the Tanakh (Genesis through Malachi) because you think that in it you have eternal life. Those very Scriptures bear witness to me, but you won't come to me in order to have life!*

> *I don't collect praise from men, but I do know you people—I know that you have no love for God in you! I have come in my Father's name, and you don't accept me; if someone else comes in his own name, him you will accept. How can you trust? You're busy collecting praise from each other, instead of seeking praise from God only.*

> *But don't think that it is I who will be your accuser before the Father. Do you know who will accuse you? Moshe, the very one you have counted on! For if you really believed Moshe, you would*

believe me; because it was about me that he wrote. But if you don't believe (hear and act upon) what he wrote, how are you going to believe what I say?" **John 5:36-37**

That same day, two of them were going toward a village about seven miles from Yerushalayim called Amma'us, and they were talking with each other about all the things that had happened.

As they talked and discussed, Yeshua himself came up and walked along with them, but something kept them from recognizing him.

He asked them, "What are you talking about with each other as you walk along?"

They stopped short, their faces downcast; and one of them, named Cleopas, answered him, "Are you the only person staying in Yerushalayim that doesn't know the things that have been going on there the last few days?"

"What things?" he asked them. They said to him, "The things about Yeshua from Natzeret. He was a prophet and proved it by the things he did and said before God and all the people. Our head cohanim (high priest) and our leaders handed him over, so that he could be sentenced to death and executed on a stake as a criminal. And we had hoped that he would be the one to liberate Isra'el! Besides all that, today is the third day since these things happened; and this morning, some of the women astounded us. They were at the tomb early and couldn't find his body, so they came back; but they also reported that they had seen a vision of angels who say he's alive! Some of our friends went to the tomb and found it exactly as the women had said, but they didn't see him."

He said to them, "Foolish people! So unwilling to put your trust in everything the prophets spoke! Didn't the Messiah have to die like this before entering his glory?"

Then, starting with Moshe and all the prophets, he explained to them the things that can be found throughout the Tanakh (Genesis through Malachi) concerning himself.

They approached the village where they were going. He made as if he were going on farther; but they held him back, saying, "Stay with us, for it's almost evening, and it's getting dark." So he went in to stay with them.

As he was reclining with them at the table, he took the matzah, made the b'rakhah (the blessing), broke it and handed it to them. Then their eyes were opened, and they recognized him. But he became invisible to them.

[Yeshua is speaking] "Not everyone who says to me, 'Lord, Lord!' will enter the Kingdom of Heaven, only those who do what my Father in heaven wants [His Instructions and Principles for His people found in the Torah, the Word of God). On that Day, many will say to me, 'Lord, Lord! Didn't we prophesy in your name? Didn't we expel demons in your name? Didn't we perform many miracles in your name?' Then I will tell them to their faces, 'I never knew you! Get away from me, you workers of lawlessness [living against or outside of the Torah]!'" **Matthew 7:21-23**

My friend, it is time to return to living in and by the lifestyle of His Kingdom again.

Chapter Five:
Preparing the Heart and
Home for Passover

We have taken a great deal into consideration concerning the question of whether we as followers of Yeshua should celebrate the King's Pesach. The decision to make Pesach a part of your life and that of your family is an important and challenging choice. For most it means leaving the Roman Christianized celebration of Easter behind as you transition to the honoring of Yeshua's death and resurrection in its proper timing and context. You are probably not going to win any popularity contests amongst other family and friends who have yet to grasp what you are grasping. However, you are going to make your Father in Heaven smile and rejoice over you. You have come home through Messiah…and now you are stepping into the lifestyle of His Household, His Kingdom! That is no little thing to Him!

Now comes putting your choice into action. There is so much to learn how to do. This might be intimidating and feel overwhelming at first. Take your time. Start simple. Create and build your family's Passover celebration over time. I promise, as time passes and you begin to step into the rhythm of the celebration and its preparations a little more each year, it will get easier. Remember that even Moses and the Israelites had a first time Passover observance too – and one far more dramatic than yours will be!

A Matter of the Heart

Preparing for the night of Passover starts with the heart. The writer of the Book of Hebrews tells us that it takes the same faith, the same trusting, that Moses had in YHVH in the first Pesach for us to receive and embrace the Pesach provided by Yeshua.

> *By trusting, Moshe, after he had grown up, refused to be called the son of Pharaoh's daughter. He chose being mistreated along with God's people rather than enjoying the passing pleasures of sin. He had come to regard abuse suffered on behalf of the Messiah as greater riches than the treasures of Egypt, for he kept his eyes fixed on the reward. By trusting, he left Egypt, not fearing the king's anger; he persevered as on who sees the unseen. By trusting, he obeyed the requirements of Pesach, including the smearing of the blood, so that the Destroyer of the firstborn would not touch the firstborn of Israel.* **Hebrews 11:24-28**

Like our spiritual ancestors, we must choose the riches of God's Kingdom over the riches of the world. We must leave our Egypt - our places of bondage - and, without fear, persevere as ones who see the unseen. We must trust that the blood of our Passover lamb meets God's requirements and protects us from the Destroyer, who seeks to take our lives. We enter the night and week of Passover with a keen awareness that YHVH has called us and set us apart from everything else in the world to be his People and spend this time with Him.

Unless we live in the land of Israel, choosing to celebrate YHVH's Feasts usually puts us at odds with work and school schedules. We must plan ahead, asking for time off from work and notifying schools that our children will be home for the Feast Days. (In Israel, schools are closed, and everyone is on holiday!) Far too many try to squeeze the Feast Days into their usual schedule, attempting to obey the command but not really entering into God's heart for us in the season. Guard *your* heart! YHVH gave this time to us for a purpose, and we must make time and space in our lives for His purpose to achieve its function in and through us. We are called to be His Light in the world. A part of being that Light is to establish His Appointed Times on earth as it is in heaven.

As with the original Passover, today's Passover is personal - household by household, person by person. It is literally a God-given opportunity to help those in our lives, especially our children and grandchildren, grasp and understand who Yeshua is, what He has accomplished for us, and what He continues to do for us. Therefore, the Passover Seder, which includes the eating of a meal, is *a family celebration* meant to be observed in the home, not at the synagogue or in a church. It is personal. It is a the celebration of our deliverance and redemption.

There are many communities of faith, both Messianic and Jewish, that include a corporate evening of celebration as an integral part of their Pesach observances. This is especially helpful for those who are unfamiliar with the traditions of the Passover Seder. Yet, I want to encourage you that if you have never experienced a night of Passover in your home, be bold, take courage, and do it. Don't stress out over doing it right. Just do it. This is a matter of the heart, not a pursuit of religious perfection. Focus on the function of the celebration – the purpose – the why. Trust me, no matter how hard you plan and try, the wine will get spilt, the lamb might get burnt, guests will not arrive on time, and perfection is impossible. Do your best. Flow with what happens or does not happen. Walk in loving obedience to our Messiah and grace toward each other. Simply enjoy the Truth and the Spirit that cannot help but permeate the evening!

Allow me to share what my husband and I have chosen for our household. We are blessed in that our congregation starts the Passover week with a celebration of Yeshua's Pesach Seder on the evening that begins Aviv 14. This is in timing with what Yeshua and those of the Pharisees did. On this night, our congregation holds a corporate Passover Seder open to the public so anyone can attend. We are encouraged to invite co-workers, employees, even friends and family to join us. The evening is catered with a Kosher unleavened meal, and the tables are beautifully set. Everyone dresses their absolute best. Together we reflect on the Passover death and resurrection of our Messiah and remember the faith of the Israelites of the Exodus. The evening is a glorious affair and is well-attended.

On the following night, the evening that begins Aviv 15, my husband and I host a family Pesach in our home. This is the traditional night of Passover, celebrated by Jews all over the world. We invite our children and grandchildren, siblings and their families, and our closest friends to join us. We have spent more than a decade crafting our celebration and it has become the highlight of the year. We fill the evening with a Seder that remembers both the Exodus and the Pesach Lamb of YHVH, Yeshua. We have a delicious meal that includes unleavened bread (matzah), bitter herbs, and roasted lamb – and we have chicken nuggets and ice cream for the little ones. We include songs for all age groups, and we weave a few Passover-themed kid's activities into the evening to keep them engaged and the parents involved in passing our heritage along to their children. If the weather is nice, we go outside and play some games. Yes, the evening is long. Yes, the kids get tired and fussy. But none of that matters. We stay relaxed and go with the flow. The key is being together in the presence of our loving King as we honor Him and remember all that He has done for us. We do what works best with our family…and as the little ones grow up and life changes, the celebration changes to meet all of us where we are at that year. We aim for purpose and function, not religious form.

The King's Instructions

The one detail we are firm about is adhering to YHVH's specific instructions for his Pesach, the Night of Nights. Take the time to become familiar with these as they are not to be ignored or left out of your celebration.

- **The day and time.** In essence, the process involved with YHVH's Pesach begins on Aviv 10 with the selection of the unblemished lamb. As mentioned earlier, the precise Night of Passover has been in debate for thousands of years. Common ground is Aviv 14 and an evening celebration into the night. Some will observe the evening beginning Aviv 14, as Yeshua did. (Keep in mind that He was focused on that target time of 3:00 PM on Aviv 14 so that the two debating parties would be without excuse concerning his sacrifice.) Others will observe the evening beginning Aviv 15. As to which night to celebrate the Passover, I have no firm answer for you. Pray. Ask the guidance of His Spirit for your household and go with what he speaks to your heart. (In saying that, do not judge others who choose differently than you.) *Exodus 12:3-7 and 23:14:-15, Leviticus 23:5, Numbers 28:16, Deuteronomy 16:1-2*

- **Specific foods.** Because the Passover sacrifice was a lamb, this is the center of most Passover meals today. Some debate that since there is no Temple to host such a sacrifice – and that Yeshua was the final Passover Lamb provided by YHVH – any meat or main dish is fine. Whatever meat you choose, it should be roasted. (Personally, we have lamb to keep with the meaningful symbolism involved.) The second food is unleavened bread, called matzah. The entire meal should be without leavening. The third specific food is maror…bitter herbs. The most used commonly used is horseradish, fresh or prepared. The tradition of wine is also important for the Seder as Yeshua used the cups of wine in the Seder to refer to his own blood being shed to seal a new covenant with Him. *Exodus 12:8-10, Deuteronomy 16:3-7*

- **The Second Passover.** In Hebrew, *Sheni Pesach.* The keeping of Passover by His People is so important to YHVH that He created a second opportunity for those who could not celebrate Passover at its appropriate time in Aviv. Sheni Passover takes place exactly one month later, on Iyar 14. There were only two reasons acceptable to YHVH for not participating in the first Passover of Aviv. The first was being in a state of uncleanness due to the *unavoidable* handling of a dead body. As in the case of Yeshua, a death in this season occasionally happens amongst our loved ones and in our community of faith. Yet, even in those cases, if handling a dead body can be avoided it should be so that your participation in Passover can take place. The second reason was due to *unavoidable* travel abroad (which in this case meant having to be outside of the land of Israel). In ancient times travel was far more involved and intense than now. Unfortunate delays were frequent. Yet, with great intensity, people did their best not to miss Passover and the week of Unleavened Bread that it welcomes. The head of the household knew that to not participate in Passover meant his household would risk going without YHVH's provision and protection in the year ahead. YHVH knew that too. Thus, he gives those who truly cannot not participate a second opportunity! On the other hand, by YHVH's decree, a person that is fully able to celebrate the first Pesach but fails to do so will be cut off from Israel. This would be the consequence for his sin (disobedience). A word to the wise should be sufficient, beloved of Yeshua. *Numbers 9:1-13*

- **The following day is a Shabbat – a Sabbath.** On this day we celebrate the departure of the Israelites from Egypt. We also remember the death of our Messiah, the Lamb of God. By date, it is Aviv 15. Yes, that old controversy over Aviv 14 is still lingering. Whatever choice you have made regarding when to celebrate the Passover Seder, make observing Aviv 15 (sunset to sunset) a day of complete rest from labor for you, your family, your livestock, your servants, and the guests in your household. YHVH has decreed that he desires a holy (uncommon and unique) assembly of His children on this day. If there isn't a Passover Sabbath service taking place near you, assemble your family and friends and create one! (Remember, it is matzah time for the next seven days! No leavened breads are to be eaten or found in your house.) *Exodus 12:14-20 and 13:3-9, Leviticus 23:6-8, Numbers 28:17-25, Deuteronomy 16:3-8*

- **Day of First Fruits – Yom HaBikkurim.** Unless it is a regular seventh-day Sabbath, the Day of First Fruits takes place on Aviv 16, the second day of the Feast of Matzah. It is not a Sabbath, yet it is an important day in the seasons and timing of the Kingdom. Throughout His Kingdom instructions,

YHVH tests the heart of loving devotion in His people regarding firsts. The first of everything belongs to Him – the firstborn of our children, the firstborn of our livestock, the first of our harvest, and the first of our increases. After the redeeming of the firstborn that takes place at Passover, the spring Day of First Fruits requires that we bring to Him, our good and perfect King, the first of the first annual crops of the land. In the land of Israel, this is the first sheaves of barley. *It would be on this day that YHVH would provide us with His first fruit offering also! On this day Yeshua rose from the dead, the First Fruit of YHVH's promised resurrections!* In the year of Yeshua's death and resurrection Aviv 16 was a regular Sabbath, so *Aviv 17 – 3 days after His Aviv 14 death – was the Day of First Fruits.* On this day (not Easter) Yeshua rose from the dead. Yes, it happened to be a Sunday that year…BUT it is *the numbering of the days* that is important to YHVH. His attention to detail in that He intentionally planned for the resurrection of His Lamb to be on the Day of First Fruits is amazing. Nothing in God's Kingdom is a coincidence. *Leviticus 23:9-14*

YHVH's instructions for His Pesach and the week that follows it are challenging, but not too difficult. There is a multitude of Jewish traditions that have become a part of these Feast Days. Some of them are very meaningful and worth considering as a part of your celebration. But they are not essential for being obedient to the Father's instructions. Some of them are based on the Mediterranean culture and lifestyle. Don't be fearful or hesitant to shape a little of your own culture into your celebration, unless such involves practices belonging to pagan gods.

In the first Passover, the night was tense. The Israelites were surrounded by the death of the firstborn of Egypt. YHVH instructed them to be fully clothed and packed so that they would be ready to leave at sunrise. Every Israelite was on edge, not sure what tomorrow would bring. No Passover was that intense again until the night of Yeshua's Passover. The firstborn Lamb of God would be the high price. The night would involve betrayal, arrest, trials, and beatings. Despite Yeshua's efforts to prepare them, the fear, shock, and sorrow Yeshua's followers experienced was immeasurable. Today we struggle to relate to the emotional and very intense reality of both Passovers. We recline at our Passover tables, relaxed and joyful. We sing songs and retell the stories. We do our best to *remez,* which is the Hebrew practice of remembering as if it were happening in this moment today. We look forward to that moment in the future when Messiah will share the cups of Passover with us, face to face. We celebrate the Season of Our Deliverance!

Time to Get Practical

Is your head now swimming in the deep waters of new knowledge? We have gone through much information and many foundational principles regarding the celebrating of Passover, the first of YHVH's annual cycle of Kingdom Feasts. Feeling a bit confused and overwhelmed is okay. Growth usually starts in that exact place. Take a deep breath! In the pages that follow I will do my best to break it all down into practical application so that you can begin to put into action what you may be struggling to wrap your head around. Take heart! I promise you that *with application will come clearer understanding.* If there is one key concept that I can get you to grasp at this moment it is this. With much of YHVH's instructions, understanding comes best by doing. Never throw your hands up and declare, "I don't get this, so I'm not going to do it!" Do not be lazy either, thinking that you will let the pastor and church leaders prepare everything and you will just show up. These are poor excuses to present to the King who looks for obedience as an action of our love and devotion to Him. Remember that YHVH wants us to celebrate His Feasts in our homes, and in His presence with our faith community. The preparation is in your hands…and leading your family in His celebrations is your responsibility. Roll up your sleeves and, with love in your heart and a smile on your face, just start! You will figure it out as you do it. I promise! Let's get started.

A Guide to Passover Preparations

The first step is to determine the month of Aviv on your calendar. You can do this a variety of ways. You can purchase an actual printed Jewish calendar online or at a synagogue. You can go online to websites for Jewish or Messianic ministries and organizations to identify the corresponding dates on our western calendar for all of the Feast Days. You may even be able to print calendars from their sites. A simple online search for *Jewish or Hebrew calendar* will give you access to an abundance of resources. Find Passover in the month of Aviv. Get out your day planner or use the calendar in your smart phone, notepad or other electronic devices and mark the dates for Rosh Chodashim (Head of the Kingdom's New Year), Passover and the Feast of Unleavened Bread. Be sure to highlight the key days of

- Aviv 1 Rosh Chodashim: the head of the Hebrew Year and the start of Passover preparations.

- Aviv 10 Shabbat HaGadol: the Great Sabbath, a day dedicated to selecting the unblemished Lamb, a day to put serious effort into preparing your heart and mind for the celebration of Passover.

- Aviv 13 If you plan to honor the timing of Yeshua's Seder, tonight is the night for your Passover celebration. If you are going to wait until the next evening, do take some time to remember what took place on this evening: Yeshua's Seder, the Garden of Gethsemane, Yeshua's arrest and trials.

- Aviv 14 This is the traditional night of Passover at the time of Yeshua and today. Today is called Preparation Day. At 3:00 PM (dusk) last-minute preparations are underway. The Passover Seder will begin just before sunset.

- Aviv 15 The Passover Sabbath and the first day of the Feast of Unleavened Bread. No matter what day of the week this falls on, this is a day of complete rest for all Israel, natural branches and those grafted in through Messiah. (Romans 11) No work and no school.

- Aviv 16 Unless this is a regular seventh-day Sabbath, this is the Day of First Fruits.

- Aviv 17 Resurrection Day! For followers of Yeshua, this is indeed a Great Sabbath of rejoicing and Celebration. No matter what day of the week this date falls on, take the day off, keep the children at home and gather with others to rejoice in our Living Messiah!

- Aviv 21 The High Sabbath of the last day of the Feast of Unleavened Bread. No matter what day of the week this falls on, this is a day of rest from all work and school. There is to be festive assembly of believers on this day in the presence of our King! As the Feast of Matzah ends at sunset, Chassidic Jews living outside of Israel celebrate what is called Mashiach's Feast (Messiah's Feast) in anticipation of His coming arrival which will bring the reuniting of the whole House of Israel, and the full restoration of YHVH's Kingdom on earth. In that same spirit of anticipation, many Messianic believers have also adopted this practice in anticipation of Yeshua HaMashiach's imminent return. This is a wonderful, prophetic evening to look forward to all that our Messiah has promised for us in our eternal future with Him. Though not commanded by our King, it is a lovely way to bring this Feast Week to full closure.

Now that you have the dates for this year's Season of Our Deliverance identified on your western calendar, you can start planning. Request days off work and let the school know which days your children will not be there.

Begin thinking about what you want to do in your home and how you can be involved in your congregation in preparing for and celebrating the Feast Days of Aviv. Below are two steps that will assist you in your preparation.

<u>Aviv 1 – 13</u>

1. **Clean your house – and your heart!**

   "Observe the month of Aviv, and keep Pesach to Adonai your God; for in the month of Aviv, YHVH your God brought you out of Egypt at night. … No leaven is to be seen with you anywhere in your territory for seven days." **Deuteronomy 16:1 & 4**

   The first two weeks of Aviv in a Hebrew home are days of intense spring cleaning! Every room, every closet, every corner, every piece of furniture and every appliance is cleaned inside and out to ensure that there isn't even the smallest crumb of leavened foods. Pockets of coats, suits, pants, and shirts are turned inside out, and the items are cleaned. Purses, backpacks, and gym bags are emptied and cleaned. Kitchen cupboards, pantry, refrigerator, and freezer are emptied of leavened foods and leavening agents. Cars are cleaned to perfection inside and out. Even storage sheds are not immune to cleaning efforts. No leaven is to be found in or on our property, owned or rented, for those seven days beginning with the night of Passover. This spring cleaning involves every member of the family as it will take a family effort to get it all done! (Many families will begin cleaning the day after Purim – the celebration of Esther's triumph – two weeks earlier.)

Looking at the Passover celebration from a heart perspective, the Apostle Paul wrote,

"Don't you know the old saying, "It takes only a little hametz to leaven the whole batch of dough?" Get rid of the old hametz, so that you can be a new batch of dough, because in reality you are unleavened. For our Pesach lamb, the Messiah has been sacrificed. So let us celebrate the Seder not with leftover hametz, the hametz of wickedness and evil, but with the matzah of purity and truth. - **I Corinthians 5:6-8**

Preparing your home for Passover (Pesach) and the Feast of Unleavened Bread (Matzah) is indeed important. However, this Passover cleaning is pointless if your life – your heart, mind, and actions – are not being cleaned out too. As you clean, make it your prayer that YHVH would help you search out the sin – the leavening that puffs up and destroys – in your life and rid yourself of it. These two weeks are in Spirit and Truth, days of repentance. The King is arriving to spend this time with you!

You want to be prepared in heart to enjoy the beauty and bounty of His Presence! The action of cleaning out your property is an outward sign of what is also happening inside of you. Teach this to your children!

A question arises for many. What exactly is hametz (chametz)? Hametz is any food that has been made from or contains a grain (wheat, barley, rye, oats, or spelt) mixed with leavening. (Leavening is any biological or chemical agent that would cause a grain to ferment or rise.) Some remove leavened foods and beverages but are at peace in leaving the actual leavening agents, such as yeast or baking powder, in their homes. Some, in strictest observance, will remove from their homes even the unmixed grains (flour, barley, rye, oats and spelt) and all leavening agents. Regardless of your choice, removing hametz requires reading labels and searching for the hidden hametz in foods and household items, even cosmetics, soaps, and cleaners. All foods and products that are hametz can be used and eaten until the Preparation Day, Aviv 14. The last of the hametz must be removed from your home that morning.

This removal of hametz seems legalistic at first. I encourage you to remember who gave this directive. Was it man or was it YHVH? God, the King, gave the directive, so now choosing to remove hametz becomes a matter of the heart. What can be become legalistic is the interpretation of how and what to remove! The extent to which you take the removal of hametz is between you and the Father. The most obvious hametz are foods and items where grains and other foods have prepared with yeast, like breads and rolls. This is the most basic and fundamental application. If you believe YHVH is asking more from you and your household then follow His lead. Whatever your household's choice, please live by one guideline – do not judge or condemn others in Messiah that have chosen a lesser or a stricter observance than you. The moment you do that you move from the position of loving personal obedience to your King into the religious legalism of the Pharisees and Sadducees. (Colossians 2:16-19)

What do we do with these leavened foods and products? Oh, how hard are the tests of our faith! This is difficult for those who have yet to learn that their provision is tied to obedience and God's Covenant promise to care our needs. Friends, trust YHVH and toss out the perishables. Give the rest to local homeless shelters, rescue shelters and food banks. Do you have folks standing on street corners in your town looking for handouts? Go ahead and bless them. It is not that difficult to find a place for your leavened foods and beverages. The difficulty lies in letting go.

To help you with your family's spring-cleaning search for hametz, here are the grains and leavening agents common to us today. Remember, hametz foods and items are those where the grain AND the leavening have been combined.

Common biological leavening agents
yeast, yeast extract
buttermilk
ginger beer
club soda
kefir
sourdough starter
yogurt
beer (contains live yeast and grain)

Chemical leavening agents
baking powder
baking soda (sodium bicarbonate)
monocalcium phosphate
sodium aluminum phosphate (SALP)
sodium acid pyrophosphate (SAPP)
other phosphates
ammonium bicarbonate (hartshorn, horn salt, bakers ammonia)
potassium bicarbonate (potash)
potassium bitartrate (cream of tartar)
potassium carbonate (pearlash)
hydrogen peroxide

Grains:
Wheat and wheat flours
Barley and barley flours
Rye and rye flours
Oats and oat flours
Spelt and spelt flours
Modified Food Starches (usually a wheat-based product unless otherwise identified)
Corn and rice are not considered grains.

For the Follower of Yeshua, Passover and the Feast of Matzah symbolize our sanctification through Messiah. This is a time where we can identify ourselves with the death and burial of Yeshua through embracing our death to sin and to our old nature. We can certainly be encouraged to remove hametz from our homes, as it is a command of our King to do so for this celebration. Yet, this is a meaningless religious act if we allow true hametz – sin infested thoughts and actions – to remain in our lives. Remember – the Biblical definition of "sin" is to miss the mark that the teachings and instructions of our Father Creator (found in the Torah) set before us. Yes, all of us do sin and fall short of the glory of God. His glory is His character, mindset, and lifestyle. His glory is revealed to us in the Torah! YHVH gives us this incredible time every year to rid our homes and our lives of spiritual darkness and choose to release His Light and blessings. What a wonderful gift the Feasts of Aviv are!

2. **Write down your plans!**

    As you approach the Feast of Aviv each year a vision will begin to form in your spirit and mind of what you want this year's celebration to look and feel like. You will know what experiences you would like to create for your children this time around. People will come to mind that you want to invite to your Seder. You will think of foods you want to serve and how you want to decorate your home. Ideas will come in helping your congregation to celebrate the season. WRITE THESE THINGS DOWN! Most of them will not happen unless you do. Make plans for what you will do and when you will do them. Assign dates and blocks of time for these vision building ideas to become a reality. Plan which days you will clean specific rooms or locations in your house. Identify the resources and items you will need to make your vision happen. Plan a shopping day to go get those items. If you realize you are going to need some help getting things done, then get help arranged. Next - *follow the plan!*

By the time Aviv 14 rolls around, you should be ready! There will perhaps be something that did not get done or did not work out as you had hoped. That is okay. Passover is going to happen anyway! Take a deep breath, release the things that did not happen, choose an attitude of joy, and jump in to enjoy this special season with our King!

Conclusion:
Passover is Something We Live

Because of Messiah Yeshua, Passover is something that we live every day, all year long. The enormous life-changing impact of the Exodus and Yeshua's Passover death and resurrection is not confined to those 7 or 8 days that we look forward to each spring. Nor are these events confined to history. What they represent and the prophecies that they fulfill are to be a part of who we are today and forever. We delight in the thought that there is a Passover yet to come when we will feast face to face with our King. Only on that day will we see and understand the full revelation of what those events mean in the scope of eternity. The Season of Our Deliverance is never-ending!

Until then, each day we are mindful that without our Deliverer-YHVH's Passover Lamb -our lives would not be what they are. The peace that passes the world's understanding would evade us. Our lives would be without hope, confusing, and without the One who created us. That, by the way, is the Hebrew definition of a pagan. The Supreme God who brought order out of chaos in creating the universe and the earth continues to create order out of chaos in our lives. Without His deep desire to be our God, we His people, and to dwell with us forever, we would not know of His grace and mercy. He is not a hard-hearted King, a God that does not care, a Father who turns us away. Passover is his heart, broken unto death to bring us home again. How can we ever forget such a great and loving Father? It is impossible.

Yeshua was once asked by a teacher of the Torah, "What are the greatest of God's commandments?" To this He replied, *"The most important is, 'Sh'ma Yisra'el, Adonai Eloheinu, Adonai echad [Hear, O Isra'el, the Lord our God, the Lord is one], and you are to love YHVH your God with all your heart, with all your soul, with all your understanding and with all your strength.' The second is this: 'You are to love your neighbor as yourself.' There is no other mitzvah (command, instruction) greater than these."* (Mark 12:29-31)

Our ability to love YHVH with all that we are rests upon embracing the Messiah and learning to walk in God's Ways. Honoring and celebrating His Sabbath and His Feast Days are outward testimony to Him (and to the world) that we love Him. We want to spend time with Him. We want to learn from Him wisdom and understanding that will make our lives and the lives of our children and grandchildren peaceful and prosperous. We do not have to do these things in some form of religious observance to pacify an angry God. On the contrary! *We want to celebrate His goodness and grace because we understand how much He loves us! We want Him to know how much we love Him in return.* Our obedience to Him is based on hearts flowing over with love in response to the love that is overflowing from Him.

It is no wonder then that YHVH calls His people his Bride! He refers to us as His betrothed wife whom He is anxiously waiting to marry and step into eternity with us. His times, His seasons, are dates with His Beloved – appointments made with the one He loves. As a dear friend of mine says, "God is not into causal dating!" I agree. He is in this for the long term. Are we? Yeshua tells us that, like a good Hebrew groom, He has gone ahead to prepare a place for us, His Bride. But every now and then He just has to spend time with us. He can't stay away! His Sabbath and Feast Days are times we can rest in His arms, breathe deeply the aroma of His Spirit, and just be with Him. We can talk about our needs with Him. We can envision with

Him our future together. We can rehearse for our Wedding Day. We can sing and dance, fully enjoying being together. We can sit close to Him and listen intently as He teaches us about life in the Kingdom and things that we will need to understand, do, and become if we are to be ones who rule by His side over his Kingdom on earth. We have an eternity together to prepare for. The Appointed Times with our King plays a life-changing role in helping us achieve that. Oh yes! When we grasp who we are to Him, we want to be deeply engaged in these incredible days together!

In the chapters of this book, we looked closely at the why behind Passover. The heart of YHVH in His Feast Days is the core to learning how to honor Him and celebrate with Him in this season. Passover was established by Him as one of His Appointed Times in which He would act on behalf of His people, *because He loves us* and *because He keeps His promises.* Our King does nothing without vision and purpose!

We barely scratched the surface of the form – the how to's – of Passover. (You will find more helpful guides in the Bonus pages of this book.) That is intentional on my part, because I want your focus to be on His heart and yours. We covered the essentials per YHVH'S instruction for the Feasts of Aviv. There is a deep well filled with Living Water in what each of his instructions represent and should mean to us. Ponder them. Search the Torah to gain insight from Him in these things. Study the Writings and the Prophets of the Tanakh (the Old Testament) to discover how these things keep appearing over and over again. YHVH works in His Kingdom and in His people through patterns. The sages call them Crimson Threads. Find those threads and follow them. They will lead you to Messiah. They will lead you into eternity with Him.

Life in Yeshua is filled with rhythm and grace. He was there with God and is God from the very beginnings of the earth. He designed life with Him to be one of rhythm and grace. His Kingdom and all that it holds is not like any kingdom created by man. But you must step in. You must go through that Passover Door and then deeply enter His Kingdom. You must choose to adapt to His Ways and enjoy His Appointed Times. Once you experience and come to treasure these as He does, you will never want to go back!

Bonus #1:
A Daily Guide to the Passover Season

The purpose of this guide is to assist and encourage you as you take a wonderful journey with our Messiah Yeshua through this season that means so very much to Him. For each date of the Passover season, you will find some foundational information for that day, reference to Jewish traditions for your consideration, suggestions for adaptations for Messianic believers, and daily Scripture readings that will help you to place the day in its Biblical context. May the Season of Our Deliverance become a rich experience you and your family will treasure every year!

There are three Sabbaths during the week of the Passover season. The first day, the last day, and the regular Sabbath that falls between them are all days of complete rest and celebration. The other days are called *intermediate days* when a light and shorter workday is encouraged. In Israel, schools and many businesses are closed for the entire week. This is Israel's spring break and most will enjoy family excursions & fun days at home.

Note: This guide follows the timing that Yeshua selected for his final Passover observance. To celebrate the Passover Seder on either night is perfectly fine. This is certainly not an issue to argue over and cause division in the body of Messiah. *The important point is that you DO celebrate Passover!* (In our household, we do both evenings. We celebrate Yeshua's Seder with our congregation on the eve of Aviv 14. Then we celebrate with family and friends in our home at sunset on Aviv 14.)

Aviv 10   Shabbat HaGadol
"The Great Sabbath", no matter which day it falls on.

In ancient Israel, today was the day that the head of each household would select a perfect, unblemished lamb for the family's Passover sacrifice and meal.

This is the day that Yeshua made His "Triumphal Entry" into Jerusalem. He was greeted by throngs of people jubilantly welcoming Him as King of the Jews and shouting "Hosanna!" which means "Save us!" They had no idea that in their actions and words they were selecting the true Passover Lamb. As Yeshua rode on the back of a young donkey into the city and toward the Temple, the selected Passover lambs for Israel were being herded into the city before Him. (Those who traveled great distances to be in Jerusalem for Passover selected and bought their perfect lambs when they arrived.) Imagine what might have been going through His thoughts on this day.

Because no Temple exists in Jerusalem at present to provide for Passover sacrifices, Jews mark this special day on the regular Sabbath preceding Passover. (This is a rabbinical tradition, not in accordance with the written Word of God.) In synagogues there are special teachings, prayers, and hymns or songs. Instructions are reviewed for preparing the home for Passover and the Feast of Matzah. Anticipation for these Holy Days is in full swing, and the excitement of seeing visiting friends and family is building.

Followers of Yeshua may want to mark the actual day – Aviv 10 – in a way that will remind us of the deep meaning of the events that took place in His life on this date. Read the corresponding Scriptures and teach your family about the significance of this day. Congregations may want to hold a special service marking the event...often called by Christians "Palm Sunday" as in the year of Yeshua's death and resurrection, the date of Aviv 10 did fall on a Sunday. Give thought and prayer to treating this day as a Sabbath (a day of rest from work and school) for your household.

Today's Scripture Readings:

Exodus 12:3-6	Isaiah 62:10-12	Zechariah 9:9
Malachi 3:4 -4:6	Psalm 118:19-29	Matthew 21:1-10
Mark 11:1-11	Luke 19:28-44	John 12:12-19

Aviv 11 and 12 Days of Preparation

During this time, the heads of the families of Israel brought their chosen lamb into their households to be cared for, carefully examined, and cleansed in preparation for the sacrifice. A personal attachment would develop between household members and the lamb. Its sacrifice would now have an emotional significance to the entire family. The mercy and grace provided by YHVH for His people through this sacrifice would have a tangible cost. The blood of their lamb would be the covering over their households for the entire year so that judgement and the penalty for sin (death) would pass over them.

It was during these same two days that Yeshua examined the Temple and declared it had become a den of thieves. The tables of the merchants and priests selling Passover lambs and other animals for sacrifice were overturned by His hands. With a whip He drove out the merchants. The crowded courts were thrown into confusion. He publicly and loudly confronted the Pharisees and Sadducees. He taught the crowds following Him about the nature of His Kingdom and the coming Day of Judgement. He healed the blind and the lame. He knew that the hour of His death was at hand and He held nothing back.

Yeshua, the Passover Lamb of YHVH, was also being examined under the watchful eye of the crowds, the religious Jewish leaders, and the Roman government. No one could find reason to condemn Him. He was found to be without spot or blemish by all three. The crowds were ready to crown Him King of Israel. The religious leaders seeking to destroy Him began to fabricate false witnesses and testimonies against Him. They created a plan to arrest and try Him during night hours when the people would be sleeping. They needed an insider who would help them in their schemes. For thirty pieces of Temple silver, Y'hudah Ben-Shi'mon from K'riot (Judas Iscariot), one of the twelve disciples closest to Yeshua, became the betrayer they sought.

During these two days make any remaining preparations for the Passover Seder and the Feast of Matzah. The house should be readied with the last of any hametz removed, Feast Days menus and activities finalized, and shopping completed.

Scripture readings during these two days:
Matthew 21:12- 22:17   Mark 11:12 – 14:10
Luke 22:1-6   John 12:20-50

Question: Which night will you celebrate the Passover?
There were two options that were practiced in Israel at the time of Yeshua. One was held by the Pharisees, who believed in the resurrection of the dead. The other was held by the Sadducees, who did not believe in the resurrection of the dead. Though both sects held power and influence over the Hebrew people, the Sadducees had full control of the Temple and the sacrifices. To accommodate both sects, Passover sacrifices began at 9:00 AM on Aviv 13 and

continued to 3:00 PM on Aviv 14. Both sects observed the Sabbath of the 1st Day of the Feast of Matzah on Aviv 15. Your choice is between you and YHVH. Choose as he leads you by His Spirit.

- At the sunset ushering in Aviv 14. This was the tradition of the Pharisees. This was the time Yeshua selected for his final Passover Seder with His disciples. He most certainly did believe in the resurrection!
- After 3:00 PM on Aviv 14. This was the tradition of the Sadducees, thus the predominate practice of the Judeans at that time. This time remains the practice of the Jews today.

Yeshua gave up his life on the stake at 3:00 PM on Aviv 14 as the last of the Passover lambs was sacrificed. At that moment, the Temple High Priest would declare, "It is finished." Our High Priest and Sacrifice declared the same at that very same moment.

A Note to the Head of the Household: *Leading the Passover Celebration is your responsibility!* Make time during these two days to read through the *Haggadah* your family is going to use as the guide for your evening of celebration. *The Haggadah* is a prepared text that gives order to all that will take place: prayers, songs, the retelling of the Exodus story and the death and resurrection of Yeshua, the eating and the breaking of the matzah and the blessings over the cups of wine. Practically speaking, your job is to be the teacher and the Haggadah is your teacher's guide. Everyone will have a copy to follow along and help them know when and how participate. Do not – repeat, *do not* – wait until the last minute to go through the Haggadah. Even worse, do not decide to wing it and go into the evening without advance thought and prayer given to what you are about to do. This is far too important a night for your family and guests, so be prepared!

Aviv 13   The Preparation Day for those holding their Passover Seder tonight

Today through Aviv 17 are remarkable days in YHVH's Kingdom! *It is highly suggested that your household take these five days off from work and school.* This will make it possible for all to fully enter the joy of this significant season and reduce the stress of trying to keep up with holiday preparations and events.

If you are celebrating the Passover Seder this evening with the arrival of Aviv 14, today you will be completing your final preparations. Check and double check your menu and list of supplies. Run those last-minute errands. Start preparing the food for your Passover meal. Involve the family in the setting of the table, preparing the Seder elements, decorating and centerpieces, and preparing the house for guests.

Today's Scripture Readings:

Exodus 12:1-32	Numbers 28:16–25	Deut. 16:1-8
Joshua 3:1 – 5:11	Matthew 26:17-29	Mark 14:12-25
Luke 22:7-38	I Corinthians 5:6-8	

The final search for hametz. Of course, by this time, the house should be completely cleansed of hametz for Passover; hopefully, there is no hametz to be found. However, there is a traditional, game-like, last search for hametz that can involve the entire family. Children love this! (This usually takes place in the morning hours of the day.)

Hametz Hide and Seek

1) Prepare ten carefully wrapped small pieces of bread and hide them throughout the house for the seekers to find.

2) At a set time of your choosing, gather the family, explain the search activity, and recite the blessing:
   Blessed are You, Yahweh our God, King of the universe, who has sanctified us by His commandments, and has commanded us concerning the removal of hametz. Amen.

3) Give each seeker a small paper bag in which to place the found hametz. Have them carefully search the entire house and collect the ten hidden pieces. Be sure to make a final count – all 10 must be found! To the one who finds the most pieces give a coin or small gift as a prize.

4) Go outside and make a small, safe fire. (Use an outdoor grill or firepit.) Burn the bags with the hametz.

5) Now proclaim what is called a nullification statement verifying that you have completed the removal of hametz and renouncing all ownership of any hametz you may have missed:
   All leaven and anything leavened that is in my possession, which I have neither seen nor removed, and about which I am unaware, shall be considered nullified and ownerless as the dust of the earth! Amen.

6) Once this game-like observance is complete, you may not eat any more hametz until after the Feast of Matzah. You are now ready to celebrate what is also called "The Feast of Freedom" for the next eight days!

Yeshua's Passover Seder took place on this evening with the sunset ushering in Aviv 14. It was of extreme importance to Yeshua to share with His disciples this important meal that is so symbolic of His death. He instructed His disciples that evening to always share the Passover Meal in remembrance of Him and what He was about to do. As His disciples today, His instruction applies to us!

Because of Yeshua's observance on this evening, many Messianic families and congregations choose to celebrate the Passover Seder on this night rather than on the traditional timing of this meal after twilight the following day. This is not an issue to argue over. To celebrate the Passover Seder on either night – or both - is perfectly fine. The important point is that you DO celebrate it!

Gethsemane: After your Seder this evening, take time to give some thought and reflection to Yeshua's last teachings and the events that took place on this night.

Evening Scripture Reading: Exodus 12:40-42 and John 13:31-18:25

Aviv 14   Crucifixion Day
Preparation Day for those observing the Passover Seder tonight

(In the Christian world the death of Yeshua is traditionally observed on Good Friday.)

It does not matter on which day of the week Aviv 14 falls on the western calendar, this is and always will be the day of Yeshua's crucifixion. Remember that Messiah's death and resurrection are to remain purposefully tied to our King's decreed Appointed Time, not that of a Roman emperor. Take today off from work and school. Make time and space in your life to honor and remember all that took place on Crucifixion Day. If you have chosen to observe your Passover Seder tonight, this will be a busy day. Give yourself the time to both prepare and remember.

The Fast of the First Born Many Jewish families observe today as a day of fasting by the first-born son of the family. This is in response to **Exodus 13:1-16** where YHVH commands the setting apart for Him of the first-born sons of Israel with a redemption sacrifice. This instruction is given within the context of Passover and the Feast of Matzah. The fast is understood to be one of thanksgiving for the sparing of the first-born sons of Israel in Egypt during the night of the very first Passover. Yeshua, first born of Mary and first born of God, indeed fasted this day while He was tried by Pilate, beaten, flogged, and crucified.

A Day of Remembrance As you move through this day, take a break at 9:00 AM and 3:00 PM to remember and honor Yeshua's death on the stake. If possible, gather your family for the reading of Scripture and prayer at each of these times. If your family enjoys singing, choose a hymn or worship song to lift to Him in remembrance and thanksgiving.

9:00 AM   This is the hour at which Yeshua was nailed on the stake at Golgotha.

Morning Scripture Readings:

Isaiah	Matthew	Luke
52:13-53:12	27:1-44	22:66 - 23:43

3:00 PM   The last sacrifice of the Passover lambs was completed in the Temple in Jerusalem. The High Priest would then declare, "It is finished!" This is the exact moment when YHVH's perfect Passover Lamb, Yeshua, proclaimed, "It is finished!", gave up His spirit, and died.

Afternoon Passover Scripture Readings:

Matthew 27:45-61   Luke 23:44-56

The 3 o'clock hour of the daily afternoon prayers, called *Minchah*, still take place every day to this day in synagogues around the world. **Psalm 145** is read aloud, and for Passover the following prayer is recited. You may want to pause for a few moments and observe this custom in remembrance of the hour of Yeshua's death.

> *Our God and God of our fathers, may there ascend, come and reach, be seen, accepted, and heard, recalled and remembered before You, the remembrance and recollection of us, the remembrance of Jerusalem Your holy city, and the remembrance of all Your people the House of Israel, for deliverance, well-being, grace, kindness, mercy, good life and peace, on this day. Remember us on this Passover, YHVH our God, for good; be mindful of us on this Passover for blessing; help us on this Passover for good life. With the promise of deliverance and compassion, spare us and be gracious to us; have mercy upon us and deliver us; for our eyes are directed to You, for You, YHVH, are a gracious and merciful King. Amen.*

Between 3:00 PM and before sunset marked the beginning of Judea's celebration of Pesach. Joseph of Arimathea requested and received Yeshua's body from Pontius Pilate. He and a handful of others placed His body in the tomb that Joseph had been preparing for his own future use.

The Night of Passover (Pesach): For millennia, Jewish families have started their Passover Seder during the 30 minutes preceding sunset. The holiday candles are lit, and the special holiday blessings are spoken in unison. According to Scripture, the Passover observance - with its beautifully crafted prayers, blessings, songs, remembrances, and delicious meal - is to be observed between sunset and complete darkness. Enjoy this special evening with those whom you call family.

During the very first night of Passover, the Israelites stayed up the entire night, vigilantly watching over their families as YHVH destroyed the first born of Egypt and ushered in Deliverance for His people. Many Jewish families and congregations honor this "night of vigil" (Exodus 12:42) by staying up all night rejoicing, dancing, and reading aloud the Exodus account.

Aviv 15 1st Day of the Feast of Matzah – The Passover Sabbath
A Day of Complete Rest - A High Shabbat

Today marks the day that Israel left the land of Egypt! Enjoy festive meals that require only light preparation. Stay in attitude of celebration and rest. Spend time enjoying family and friends in celebration of our freedom in Messiah.

This is, by YHVH's instruction, also a day of holy assembly so be sure to seek out a local Messianic congregation that you can worship with. If one is not available, be encouraged to gather fellow followers of Yeshua in your home for a special time of worship. Spend some meaningful time in union with each other and with our Father today. Think about what the disciples of Yeshua might have been thinking, feeling, and doing on this day after the death of Messiah.

At sunset, The Day of First Fruits begins. Have you yet presented a Passover offering to YHVH? If not, this evening and tomorrow is the time to be sure you do. This Passover season is one of the three appointed times that the King of the Universe instructs that we are not to come before him emptyhanded. The Feast seasons correspond with times of harvest in the land of Israel. The offerings given during the Feast seasons are called *voluntary offerings*, meaning that how much you choose to give as the first fruits of your season's harvest (increase) is up to you, as long as it is in accordance with the provision and increase YHVH has blessed you with.

Today's Scripture Readings:
Exodus 12:34-41 & 13:17-22 II Kings 23:1-30 Matthew 27:62-66

Aviv 16   Feast of Matzah Day 2 - The Day of First Fruits (Yom HaBikkurim)

In the year of Yeshua's death, this date fell on a regular Sabbath. Coupled with the previous day's Passover Sabbath, it would be yet another day before the women could go to the tomb to properly anoint His body to complete His burial.

Unless this is a regular seventh-day Sabbath, today is the Day of First Fruits.

A noticeably light workload is acceptable today, as we keep in mind that this day is especially important to the week called Passover. The mood remains festive and the focus is on thanksgiving to our Father for His provision and increase in all areas of our lives. If you can take the day off from work completely, do so.

Today's Scripture Readings:
Leviticus 23:9-16   I Corinthians 15:20-23   James 1:17-20

In ancient times, this day was one of celebration and thanking God for the first of the spring harvest in Israel. Sheaves of barley were waved in the Temple by the priests as part of the offerings from the people. Then they would dedicate the harvests yet to come in this year to Him and ask for His blessings, favor, and protection over their households, fields, trades, and businesses. Again, if you have not yet presented an offering in this Passover season, this is the day to see to it. This is the first of your spring harvest (increase), the first harvest (increase) in the Kingdom's New Year. Give in anticipation of what is yet to come!

Yeshua's First Fruit Resurrection

In that particular year, a regular Sabbath separated the Passover Sabbath and the Day of First Fruits. (A double blessing!) Thus, sometime between tonight's sunset and tomorrow's sunrise, in the early hours of Aviv 17, Yeshua rose from the dead! It is no coincidence that His resurrection happened in connection with the Feast of First Fruits as He is, by God's design, the First Fruit of the resurrected. His resurrection marked the beginning a great worldwide harvest of souls for the Kingdom of God. His resurrection is our sealed promise and hope for our own resurrection in the future!

Aviv 17   Feast of Matzah Day 3: The True Resurrection Day!

(In the Christian world Yeshua's resurrection is celebrated on Easter Sunday.)

It was after the observance of two Sabbath days that on this morning, the Day of First Fruits in that year, the disciples discovered the overnight resurrection of Yeshua!

Of all the days of the year, THIS is the day to have your household take off from work and school to REJOICE! It does not matter on which day of the week Aviv 17 falls in our western calendar, this is Resurrection Day! We are to always remember that Yeshua's death and resurrection are to remain purposefully tied to our King's decreed Appointed Time, not that of a Roman emperor.

Gather with friends and family for a joyful day of celebration – sing, dance, enjoy festive foods and praise our Messiah with wholeheartedness! Imagine how the disciples must have felt on that day! If you had been there, how would you have responded?

Today's Scripture Readings:
Genesis 3:14-15   John 20 & 21
Acts 2:22-36   Psalm 113

SPECIAL NOTE:

The Regular Sabbath during the Feast of Unleavened Bread: A regular seventh-day Shabbat will usually take place at some point during the week of Matzah. Because this Shabbat is a part of the Feast Week, it is an extra special day of rest and joyful celebration. Make this a special Sabbath celebration for your family. Attend Shabbat services at your local Messianic fellowship to continue to rejoice in union together in this Season of Our Deliverance.

Feast of Matzah regular weekly Shabbat Readings:
In addition to the regular weekly Torah and Haftarah readings:
Exodus 33:12 - 34:35   Ezekiel 36:16 - 37:28

Aviv 18   Feast of Matzah Day 4

<u>Unless it is Shabbat, this is an intermediate day</u> when a light and shorter workday is encouraged. Stay in a festive attitude and enjoy a fun activity with family and friends! (In Israel: Schools are on holiday & most businesses, if open, will close early.)

Today's Scripture Readings:
II Chronicles 30   Matthew 28   Psalm 114

Aviv 19   Feast of Matzah Day 5

Unless it is Shabbat, this is an intermediate day when a light and shorter workday is encouraged. Stay in a festive attitude and enjoy a fun activity with family and friends! (In Israel: Schools are on holiday & most businesses, if open, will close early.)

Today's Scripture Readings:
Ezra 6:1-22   Mark 16   Psalm 115

Aviv 20   Feast of Matzah Day 6

Unless it is Shabbat, this is an intermediate day when a light and shorter workday is encouraged. Stay in a festive attitude and enjoy a fun activity with family and friends! (In Israel: Schools are on holiday & most businesses, if open, will close early.)

Today's Scripture Readings:
II Samuel 22:1-51 Psalm 116   Luke 24:13-53

This is also a Preparation Day for the final day the Feast of Matzah, which by YHVH's decree is a Sabbath (no matter what day of the week it falls on the western calendar). This High Sabbath will begin as sunset this evening. Be sure to prepare food for meals tomorrow so that the day been full of rest and celebration. If your family is planning to celebrate Mashiach's Feast (see below) tomorrow evening at the close of the Feast Week, be sure to include preparation for this event in today's efforts.

On this High Sabbath evening we commemorate the Splitting of the Red Sea. The meal should be festive as we remember this mighty event which took place during the night. Consider what special foods, table decorations, and activities you can make a part of your evening celebration as we remember this awesome act of our King.

Evening Reading:
Deuteronomy 16:1-17   Exodus 13:17-15:26

Aviv 21 Feast of Matzah Day 7 The 2nd High Sabbath of Passover Week

No matter what day of the week it is on the western calendar, today is day of complete rest and celebration for our households! Lunch should be festive yet easy to prepare. By our King's decree, this is a day of holy assembly. Messianic and Jewish congregations will hold special services. Be sure to attend! If no such service is available to you, gather fellow followers of Yeshua for a special time of worship in your home or a selected location. Spend some special time in union with each other and our Father YHVH today.

Today's High Sabbath Scripture Readings:

Deuteronomy 16:1-17	Matthew 24:31-46
Acts 1:1-11	Psalm 117

Mashiach's Feast is this evening. As the Passover week of the Feast of Matzah ends at sunset, Chassidic Jews living outside of Israel celebrate what is called Mashiach's Feast (Messiah's Feast) in anticipation of His coming arrival which will bring the reuniting of the whole House of Israel, and the full restoration of YHVH's Kingdom on earth. In that same spirit of anticipation, many Messianic believers have also adopted this practice in anticipation of Yeshua HaMashiach's imminent return. Did YHVH command that this feast take place? No, it is a human tradition – but one of good purpose and meaning. Mashiach's Feast points us forward into our future and is a lovely way to bring the Feast Week to full closure.

The celebration serves the same function as a regular Shabbat evening Havdalah ceremony, in that is brings this appointed and holy time of the Feast of Matzah to a close. Similar to the Passover Seder, the meal includes bread (fresh leavened bread!) and four cups of wine, each representing the promises of God found in Exodus 6: a Cup of Remembrance, a Cup of Deliverance, a Cup of Sanctification, and a Cup of Inheritance. Should you choose to have a Mashiach's Feast in your household, use this evening to celebrate and look forward to the imminent return of Yeshua, the coming redemption of all Israel, and the restoration of YHVH's Kingdom on earth under Messiah's reign. (A suggested guide to this celebration is included in this book. You are welcome to use it as is, or as a guide to create your own unique celebration.)

Aviv 22 Feast of Matzah	Celebrated outside the land of Israel –
Day 8	a High Sabbath

For many centuries now, Jews living outside the land of Israel celebrate holy days for an additional day. In ancient days there was no set calendar for the Jewish people. Everything was timed based on a proclamation from the Temple priests at the sighting of the new moon each month (called Rosh Chodesh). In the early Diaspora years (since 70 AD) Temple messengers were no longer able to get the announcement to Jews outside Israel in time for the proper setting of Feast celebrations. Therefore, it was decided to extend all feast celebrations an additional day for those outside of the land to ensure the correct day had not been missed. Though today we have calendars by which to mark and set the passage of each day and month, a rabbinical decision was made to keep to the second day formula.

To observe this Eighth Day Sabbath of Passover Week is up to you and your household.

Like the day seven High Sabbath yesterday, there is no work today. Lunch should be festive and fun. Our attitude and activities should continue to be joyous and in celebration of The Season of Our Deliverance.

Bonus #2:
A Hebrew Passover Seder Haggadah for Followers of Yeshua

<u>Preparing for Your Passover Seder</u>

Items You Will Need:
- 2 candles with candlesticks
- Lighter or matches
- A Passover Seder Plate is desirable to display of all of the elements: lamb shank or rib bone, parsley, horseradish, and Charoset (a delicious mixture of apples, honey, and sometimes nuts) - possibly make this a part of your centerpiece (You can easily find Charoset recipes online.)
- An empty wine goblet for Elijah's Cup – possibly make it part of your centerpiece
- A wine goblet for each guest
- A basin of clean water (for washing of hands)
- A small, clean hand towel – cloth or paper – one for each guest
- A large napkin or Matzah Tosh in which 3 unbroken pieces of matzah are place – set at the Leader's place setting AND a large napkin for hiding the Afikomen (see Seder text)
- A nice prize for one child – a few coins or a toy or some candies in a nice little gift bag
- 4 notecards with one of the Four Questions – give these to the child or children who will be asking the Leaders these questions. (see Seder text)
- A copy of the Passover Seder Haggadah for each guest

- Copies of the lyrics to the praise & worship songs you select – one for each guest. You might want to consider using music videos with lyrics to enhance or help in this part of your celebration.
- Passover coloring pages & crayons or other quiet activities for children (You can find online coloring pages depicting the Exodus and the Passover events of Yeshua's life.)

Special Foods:
- A red wine (or grape juice) for adults
- Grape juice for children (Use sparkling grape juice as special beverage for the children!)
- Plate or basket of Matzah (unleavened bread) – be generous, this is to serve everyone!
- Butter
- One lamb shank or rib bone (should be baked and cleaned)
- Charoset – a mixture of finely chopped apples, honey, and wine/grape juice (There are many recipes online – choose one that appeals to you!)
- Small sprigs of fresh parsley – one for each guest
- Horseradish (bitter herb)
- Any condiments you will need for your main Passover meal
- Because the meal is not served until later in the evening, have some simple appetizers and beverages available for your guests (especially the children) as they arrive.

Each place setting for your guests should have:
- A goblet with a small portion of wine or juice.
- Salad or dessert plate with the following items: spring of parsley, generous scoop of Charoset, tablespoon of horseradish

- A small bowl of salt water (or a small bowl that can be shared by 2 or 3 guests (for dipping parsley)
- Cloth or paper hand towel for drying hands

Passover Meal Menu Suggestions

Remember – no leavening can be used in your menu!

- Lamb is preferred with Roast Chicken, Short Ribs, Salmon, or Brisket as other options
- Matzo Ball Soup (chicken broth based)
- Roasted Vegetables and/or Salads
- Potatoes or Sweet Potatoes
- Macaroons or some other type of unleavened dessert
- Plenty of matzah with butter, hummus, or other types of toppings
- Wines/beverages that will compliment your dinner menu
- Be sure to have unleavened foods that children can eat if they are not partial to the adult menu!

A Hebrew Passover Seder Haggadah for Followers of Yeshua

A Welcome and Introduction to the Evening

Leader: We welcome each of you to our Pesach Seder (Passover Service)! By YHVH's (Yahweh) design Passover is to be celebrated household by household throughout the Kingdom of His children, so we thank you for joining us in our household on this incredibly special evening.

On the table set before us, you see some items and settings that are unique to a Passover celebration. The partially filled glass of wine/juice at your setting is for just a few moments from now, so please do not drink it yet! Before you there is also a small plate with parsley, an apple mixture called Charoset, and some horseradish. Please do not eat these until we reach the moments in our evening in which each item will be used. You also see a small bowl of water. This water is very salty and will be used at a specific point in our evening.

For the children, there are activities prepared that will help them enjoy this evening. We do not expect them to sit perfectly still. They are children, so let them be children - under adult supervision of course! The Passover Seder can become a long ordeal for the little ones, so please allow them to be comfortable with as we journey along. They are welcome to sit on the floor (or at a nearby children's table) ... just keep them within hearing distance and encourage them to remain somewhat quiet. They will still absorb more than you might think!

At your setting you also see a Passover Seder Haggadah. This is for you to follow along with our celebration and will be your helpful companion this evening. There are numerous places throughout the evening in which you will be asked to participate. This is true for the children too. This guide contains those details for you. The word *Haggadah* means *the telling*. In His instructions for Passover, YHVH instructs us that we are retell the story of the Exodus every year, teaching our children of its importance to us as His people. This is how we are to remember *YHVH* this evening. Because our Messiah's death and resurrection was the prophetic fulfillment of Passover, we also retell the story of His last Passover Seder, His crucifixion, and His resurrection. This is in response to Yeshua's instruction that we do this in remembrance in him. The Passover Seder Haggadah guides us through *the telling* and gives order to our evening as well.

For those who are new to and unfamiliar with Passover, we are going to take a couple of moments to help you understand this special night in the context which our Heavenly Father gave it to us. Passover is important to him and it is important that we do our best to grasp its fullest meaning.

Tonight is the Night of Passover and the beginning of the Feast of Unleavened Bread, which includes the Day of First Fruits. This week of Feasts holds the first three of the annual Seven Feasts of YHVH El Elyon...Yahweh God Most High. The Feasts, sometimes called Festivals, were appointed by YHVH at specific times of the year in His Kingdom that He desires to meet with us, anoint us, and open the windows of heaven for short seasons of blessing for His people who are called by His name. His Feast days give us, as the citizens of His Kingdom, reason to step away from our hurried lives to remember who we are and to whom we belong. This evening we join both Jews and Christians around the world who are celebrating Passover no matter where life has placed them. We look forward to the day when we will celebrate Passover together in His Presence, fully united as One New Man in Messiah.

Throughout the Bible, Yahweh tells us to remember. His Feast Days always focus on remembering. What are we remembering tonight?

1. We are remembering the first great Passover that ushered in the deliverance and salvation of Israel from their slavery to Egypt.
2. We are remembering the second great Passover when Yeshua (Jesus) celebrated His Passover with His disciples,

then died for us to deliver us from our slavery to the bondages that exist in our own lives.

3. We are also remembering that there will be a future Passover when Yeshua returns and promises to share His great Passover Seder with us again!

In Exodus 12:11-14 YHVH instructed the Hebrew people regarding the first Passover:

(We are using the Complete Jewish Bible tonight.)

> *"Here is how you are to eat it (the Passover meal): with your belt fastened, your shoes on your feet and your staff in your hand; and you are to eat it hurriedly. It is YHVH's Pesach [literally: to skip or jump; between the two evenings]." For that night, I will pass through the land of Egypt and kill all the firstborn of the land of Egypt, both men and animals; and I will execute judgement against all the gods of Egypt; I am YHVH. The blood will serve you as a sign marking the houses where you are; when I see the blood, I will pass pasach [pass over] you – when I strike the land of Egypt, the death blow will not strike you. This will be a day to for you to remember and celebrate as a festival to YHVH; from generation to generation, you are to celebrate it by a perpetual (never ending) regulation."*

Yahweh instructed His people to forever remember and celebrate His Passover with roasted lamb, matzah (unleavened bread) and maror (bitter herbs). Over the centuries, other items have been added to the Passover Seder, each bearing a significance drawn from the history of the Hebrew people. However, YHVH requires only these three. In our Passover Seder we have chosen to include two of the additional items – parsley and Charoset - because they are great reminders of YHVH's faithfulness to His people.

The Bible makes it clear that Yeshua (Jesus) our Messiah was a Hebrew man, of the tribe of Judah. As a child, He traveled with His parents to celebrate Passover in Jerusalem and continued to celebrate Passover all His life. In the New Testament, all four of the Gospels tell us about what Christians call "the Last Supper". This last meal Yeshua shared with His disciples before His arrest, trial, and crucifixion was a Passover Seder! Let's read aloud together the account as it is found in Luke 22:1-15.

The festival of Unleavened Bread (matzah), known as Passover, was approaching; and the head priests and the Torah-teachers began trying to find some way to get rid of Yeshua (Jesus), because they were afraid of the people. At this point the Adversary went into Judas from K'riot, who was one of the Twelve. He approached the head priests and the Temple guard and discussed with them how he might turn Yeshua over to them. They were pleased and offered to pay him money. Judas agreed and began looking for a good opportunity to betray Yeshua without the people's knowledge. ...

Then came the day of matzah, on which the Passover lamb had to be killed. Yeshua sent Peter and John, instructing them, "Go and prepare our Passover Seder, so we can eat." They asked him, "Where do you want us to prepare it?" He told them, "As you're going into the city, a man carrying a jar of water will meet you. Follow him into the house he enters, and say to its owner, 'The Rabbi says to you, "Where is the guest room, where I am to eat the Pesach meal with my talmidim [disciples]?" 'He will show you a large room upstairs already furnished; make the preparations there." They went and found things just as Yeshua had told them they would be, and they prepared for the Seder.

When the time came, Yeshua and the disciples reclined at the Passover table and He said to them, *"I have really wanted so much to celebrate this Seder with you before I die! For I tell you, it is certain that I will not celebrate it again until it is given its full meaning in the Kingdom of God."* In the future, will He celebrate Passover again with us, face to face? Yes, He will!

Later that evening Yeshua was arrested and then tried by both Jews and Romans through the night hours. On the following day, Yeshua gave up His life as YHVH's perfect, unblemished Passover Lamb. His blood was shed so that any who call upon Him for deliverance shall be saved from living in an eternal kingdom of Darkness and Death. At that very moment of embracing the Messiah and confessing to the world that He is our God and King, we cross over to living in His eternal Kingdom of Light and Life. Praise YHVH for His deliverance!

The early believers continued to celebrate YHVH's Passover with an understanding that they were a continuation of the people of Israel. The Apostle Paul tells us in Romans 11: 17-18 that all followers of Yeshua the Messiah, Jew and Gentile, are a part of a reunited whole House of Israel. We are no longer separated from God or from each other. We have become the one new man, the one stick in the hand of one true Shepherd, just as Ezekiel foretold. (Ezekiel 37) Through trust in Yeshua as our Deliverer and King, we have become descendants of Abraham, Isaac, and Jacob. We are citizens of YHVH's Kingdom and are no longer foreigners to the promises of His Covenant with His people, Israel.

For the Jewish believer, this is true both by ethnic heritage and by trusting in Yeshua as the promised Messiah. For the non-Jewish believer, this is true because trusting in Yeshua grafts them into

Israel as adopted sons and daughters. Both become true citizens of Israel and a part of YHVH's royal family. From the moment of Yeshua's death YHVH made it possible for Jews *and* non-Jews to be brought together as one in the Messiah. Together we have become the betrothed Bride of our King Yeshua.

This evening, in this very moment, we join many believers worldwide who have chosen to continue to follow YHVH's instruction to never abandon the Feasts of His Kingdom. Tonight, we welcome Passover, the Feast of Unleavened Bread, and the Feast of First Fruits into our home and into our lives. We chose to rejoice in what is called the Season of Our Deliverance!

As we move through our Passover Seder this evening, we will be speaking prayers and blessings regarding Yahweh's faithfulness to us and the uniqueness of our relationship with Him. Each is a reminder of who Yahweh is to us, what He is faithfully doing for us, and what our loving response to Him is always to be. You are invited to speak them with us!

In truth, without the Passover sacrifice of Yeshua, all of us would still be in slavery to this world. Therefore, we encourage you to make tonight's Passover Seder a celebration of your Season of Deliverance…for YHVH is the same yesterday, today and forever!

Let us Begin the Celebration!

Candle Lighting

Leader: We start our celebration this evening by asking the matriarch of this household to light the candles of Passover, symbolizing the arrival of Messiah's light to our table. By lighting these candles, we separate ourselves and our home from the darkness of the world around us and step fully into the light of His Kingdom as we celebrate this special season with Him.

A woman lights the holiday candles, right to left, and speaks the Holy Day blessings:

> Over the 1st Candle: *Blessed are You, Yahweh our God, King of the Universe, who has granted us life, sustained us, and enabled us to reach this occasion. Amen.*

> Over the 2nd candle: *Blessed are You, Yahweh our God, King of the Universe, who has sanctified us with Your Word and given us Yeshua our Messiah, and who has commanded us to be His Light to the world. Amen.*

Leader: Together in spoken prayer, we proclaim:

> *Father, as we light these candles for Passover, we declare tonight and the next 7 days to be a holy time set aside for you. We ask you to shed your light, your miracles, all your promises, your goodness, and your joy into our lives, families, and homes during this special time. We love you so much and thank you for giving us, as your Bride, the great gift of this special evening together with you. Amen.*

The First Cup of Passover – The Cup of Sanctification

Leader: Tonight, we will partake of four cups of wine (or grape juice). Each cup holds a specific meaning, which we will reveal as we go along. Everyone, please lift the First Cup with your right hand and hold it. This is the Cup of Sanctification. Sanctification means "the setting apart". With this cup, we remember that YHVH

(Yahweh) delivered Israel from their bondage to Egypt to set them apart as His people. Together let's read aloud His Word.

> *"Therefore say to the children of Israel: I am YHVH; <u>I will bring you out</u> from under the burdens of the Egyptians, I will rescue you from their bondage, and I will redeem you with an outstretched arm and with great judgments. I will take you as My people, and I will be your God."* **Exodus 6.6-7**

Yeshua also shared the Cup of Sanctification with His disciples the night before His death. Let's read aloud.

> *Then, taking a cup of wine, he made the blessing and said, "Take this and share it among yourselves."* **Luke 22:17**

The Cup of Sanctification is also a symbol of freedom. As we drink this cup, we are reminded of the freedom that is ours because of our deliverance through our Messiah from our bondages to the corrupt systems and unrighteous ways of the world.

Please join me in speaking this prayer and the blessing over the First Cup of Passover – the Cup of Sanctification.

> *Father, tonight we are reminded by this Cup of Sanctification that it is only by the blood of Yeshua that we can be free from the brutal bondages of life outside of Your Kingdom and Your Ways. Let this Cup also remind us that we are sanctified. You have brought us out from under the burden of our sin that separated us from You. Because of your Passover Lamb, we have been set apart to be the children of the Living God, your special treasure, on this earth. Because of this great Truth, every one of us has the right to come before your throne to have our prayers not only heard but answered. No longer can anyone, especially our enemy Satan, tell*

us we are unworthy. Yeshua has made us worthy! Yahweh, we gratefully rejoice in this truth tonight. Thank you, Father! Blessed are You, Yahweh our God, King of the Universe, who creates the fruit of the vine. Amen.

Everyone drinks the First Cup of Passover. (And refills for the next Cup!)

The Washing of Hands

Leader: The washing of our hands is a reminder of the act of purification. Washing our hands indicates that we desire our hearts and our lives to be pure before God. When we wash our hands, we wash away all the things of the world, our impure thoughts, and any bad attitudes that have weighed us down. In the days of the Temple, the priests had to wash their hands before they offered sacrifices or entered the Holy of Holies. Yeshua tells us that through him we have become the priests and kings of his Kingdom. Join me in reading aloud from a Psalm of King David.

Who may go up to the mountain of Yahweh? Who can stand in his holy place? Those with clean hands and pure hearts, who don't make vanities the purpose of their lives or swear oaths just to deceive. They will receive a blessing and justice from Yahweh, who saves them. **Psalm 24: 3-5**

According to John 13, it was at this point in Yeshua's Passover Seder that He changed things up a little. After the washing of the hands, Yeshua knelt before each of His disciples and washed their feet. Imagine how surprised they were at His actions! He did this as a humble expression of His love for them, and as an example to them of the attitude of service required to be a leader in His Kingdom. In those days, the washing of feet always included anointing the feet with oil and indicated that the one doing the washing is willing to lay down his life for his guest. The laying down of one's life for another is the deepest meaning of being in covenant with each other. Please join me in speaking this prayer and the blessing over the washing of hands.

> *Father, tonight we wash our hands as a symbol of the pureness of our hearts. We thank you for the sacrifice of Yeshua that makes it possible for us to stand cleanly in your presence and to walk in love, service, and humility toward each other. Blessed are You, Yahweh our God, King of the Universe. You have sanctified us by Your Commandments and commanded us regarding the washing of our hands and hearts. Amen.*

In an attitude of love, humility, and service, let's help each other wash our hands.

The Parsley

Leader: Let each of us take a sprig of parsley. The parsley is to remind us that when the spirit of death was approaching the people of Israel, they dipped hyssop branches in the blood of their sacrificed Passover lamb and put it on the door posts of their home. The blood on the door posts told YHVH (Yahweh) that those inside were obedient and loyal to Him. He could stand in their threshold as the Door that protected them while the Death Angel passed over Egypt to kill the firstborn. Tonight, we are reminded that it is important for us to remember every day that Yeshua, our perfect Passover Lamb, shed his blood to protect and deliver us from eternal death.

We now dip our parsley into the bowl of salt water. The saltiness of the water reminds us of the bitter, salty tears the Israelites shed because of the suffering they endured as slaves. This salty water also reminds us of the bitter tears that we shed before we were delivered -- before we knew Yeshua as the Son of Living God, the King of Kings, and the Lord of Lords. Please join me in speaking this prayer and the blessing over the parsley.

Father, we thank you of this reminder of Your promise that no matter what is coming at us in this world – be it the threat of sickness, diseases, divorce, poverty, or anything else – that threat will see over our lives the blood of Yeshua, our Passover Lamb, and know that it cannot enter our house. Blessed are You, Yahweh our God, King of the Universe, who creates the fruit of the earth. Amen.

Everyone dip and eat the parsley.

The Unleavened Bread

The Leader holds up takes the napkin (or the matzah tosh) with the 3 pieces of matzah so that all can see. Open the wrapping and reveal the matzah.

Leader: This is the unleavened bread of Passover and the Feast of Unleavened Bread. In Hebrew it is called matzah. First, I am going to remove this center piece. Now I am going to break this middle piece of matzah into two pieces. The larger piece I am wrapping in a large napkin. This piece is called the *Afikomen*, which means *what comes later*. As head of our Seder this evening, I am going to hide the Afikomen and the children will get the chance to try to find it later this evening. The one who finds it will receive a prize! Children close your eyes! No peeking! I will now hide the Afikomen.

The Leader hides the Afikomen and returns to the table.

Leader: (*hold up the remaining half of the broken matzah*) On Passover and during the 7 days of the Feast of Unleavened Bread we eat only matzah, no other breads. This is a flatbread made without yeast and is symbolic of our forefather's quick exodus. They had to leave Egypt so quickly that they did not have time for their bread dough to rise before baking. In the Torah, Yahweh commands us that prior to these seven days we are to remove all leavenings and foods containing leavening from our homes. During this Feast Week we eat only matzah with our meals.

Leaven, usually meaning yeast, is often used in the Bible as a metaphor for the bad influence of sin in our lives. Sin is our actions – or lack of actions – in disobedience to God's instructions in His Word, which is the Torah. When we choose to follow Yeshua, we choose to get rid of the leavening of sin in our lives. We chose to learn of God's Ways and live by them. Let's read aloud together what the Apostle Paul instructs us in I Corinthians 5:6-8.

> *Don't you know the saying, 'It takes only a little chametz [yeast] to leaven a whole batch of dough?' Get rid of the old chametz, so that you can be a brand new batch of dough, because in reality you are unleavened [without sin]. For our Passover Lamb, the Messiah has been sacrificed! So let us celebrate the Seder not with leftover chametz, the chametz of wickedness and evil, but with the matzah of purity and truth.*

Matzah is called "the bread of affliction" and reminds us of the suffering of our ancestors as slaves. Notice the stripes and piercings that represent the terrible beatings suffered by the Israelites. This bread of affliction also reminds us that Yeshua suffered for our sin. Notice the stripes and piercings that remind us of how he was wounded for us. This was not a coincidence, but the fulfilling of prophecy concerning Israel's Messiah. Let's read the prophecy together.

> *In fact, it was our diseases he bore, our pains from which he suffered; yet we regarded him as punished, stricken and afflicted by God. But he was wounded because of our crimes, crushed because of our sins; the disciplining that makes us whole fell on him, and by his bruises we are healed.* **Isaiah 53:4-5**

Leader: I am now placing the half piece of broken matzah back into the napkin, placing it between the two remaining whole matzahs. This action symbolizes the placing of Yeshua's bruised and lifeless body in the tomb carved in stone.

Telling the Story

Note to leaders. Here are some creative suggestions in how to bring the Bible text to life for young children:

- *Use a Bible storybook or Bible video that tells the story of the Exodus in a form they will enjoy and easily understand. (Check for resources online.)*
- *Using puppets or toy figures is also a fun way to tell the story.*
- *Songs are also a good storytelling method. Insert some into a simple telling of the account.*
- *If time for preparation by the children is available in the days before Passover, simple skits can also be used to tell the story.*

Leader: We have reached the point in the evening where we recount the story of the first Passover that took place in Egypt so many centuries ago. We want all the children involved, so let's get them all comfortably seated at the table with us. (Pause as long as necessary.) We are going to read the Exodus account as recorded in the Bible. Below are the verses. I am going to ask some of you to be our readers! (Include older children and teens as readers.)

Reader 1: Exodus 11:1-10 *Yahweh said to Moshe, "I'm going to bring still one more plague on Pharaoh and Egypt, and after that he will let you leave here. When he does let you go, he will throw you out completely! Now tell the people that every man is to ask his neighbor and every woman her neighbor for gold and silver jewelry." Yahweh made the Egyptians favorably disposed toward the people. Moreover, Moshe was regarded by Pharaoh's servants and the people as a very great man in the land of Egypt. Moshe said, "Here is what Yahweh says: 'About midnight I will go out into Egypt, and all the firstborn in the land of Egypt will die, from the firstborn of Pharaoh sitting on his throne to the firstborn of the slave-girl at the handmill, and all the firstborn of the livestock. There will be a horrendous wailing throughout all the land of Egypt—there has never been another like it, and there never will be again. But not even a dog's growl will be heard against any of the people of Isra'el, neither against people nor against animals. In this way you will realize that Yahweh distinguishes between Egyptians and Isra'el. All your servants will come down to me, prostrate themselves before me and say, "Get out!— you and all the people who follow you!" and after that, I will go out!' "And he went out from Pharaoh in the heat of anger. Yahweh said to Moshe, "Pharaoh will not listen to you, so that still more of my wonders will be shown in the land of Egypt." Moshe and Aharon did all these wonders before Pharaoh, but Yahweh had made Pharaoh hardhearted, and he didn't let the people of Isra'el leave his land.*

Reader 2: Exodus 12:1-13 *Yahweh spoke to Moshe and Aharon in the land of Egypt; he said, "You are to begin your calendar with this month; it will be the first month of the year for you. Speak to all the assembly of Isra'el and say, 'On the tenth day of this month, each man* *is to take a lamb or kid for his family, one per household—except that if the household is too small for a whole lamb or kid, then he and his next-door neighbor should share one, dividing it in proportion to the number of people eating it. Your animal must be without defect, a male in its first year, and you may choose it from either the sheep or the goats. You are to keep it until the fourteenth day of the month, and then the entire assembly of the community of Isra'el will slaughter it at dusk. They are to take some of the blood and smear it on the two sides and top of the door-frame at the entrance of the house in which they eat it. That night, they are to eat the meat, roasted in the fire; they are to eat it with matzah and maror. Don't eat it raw or boiled, but roasted in the fire, with its head, the lower parts of its legs and its inner organs. Let nothing of it remain till morning; if any of it does remain, burn it up completely. Here is how you are to eat it: with your belt fastened, your shoes on your feet and your staff in your hand; and you are to eat it hurriedly. It is Yahweh's Pesach [Passover]. For that night, I will pass through the land of Egypt and kill all the firstborn in the land of Egypt, both men and animals; and I will execute judgment against all the gods of Egypt; I am Yahweh. The blood will serve you as a sign marking the houses where you are; when I see the blood, I will pass over [Hebrew: pasach] you—when I strike the land of Egypt, the death blow will not strike you."*

Reader 3: Exodus 12:14-24 *(Yahweh continues speaking)* *"This will be a day for you to remember and celebrate as a festival to Yahweh; from generation to generation you are to celebrate it by a perpetual regulation. For seven days you are to eat matzah—on the first day remove the leaven from your houses. For whoever eats hametz [leavened bread] from the first to the seventh day is to be cut off from Isra'el. On the first and seventh days, you are to have an assembly set aside for God. On these days no work is to be done, except what each* *must do to prepare his food; you may do only that. You are to observe the festival of matzah, for on this very day I brought your divisions out of the land of Egypt. Therefore, you are to observe this day from generation to generation by a perpetual regulation. From the evening of the fourteenth day of the first month until the evening of the twenty-first day, you are to eat matzah. During those seven days, no leaven is to be found in your houses. Whoever eats food with hametz in it is to be cut off from the community of Isra'el—it doesn't matter whether he is a foreigner or a citizen of the land. Eat nothing with hametz in it. Wherever you live, eat matzah." Then Moshe called for all the leaders of Isra'el and said, "Select and take lambs for your families, and slaughter the Pesach lamb. Take a bunch of hyssop leaves and dip it in the blood which is in the basin, and smear it on the two sides and top of the door-frame. Then, none of you is to go out the door of his house until morning. For Yahweh will pass through to kill the Egyptians; but when he sees the blood on the top and on the two sides, Yahweh will pass over the door and will not allow the Slaughterer to enter your houses and kill you. You are to observe this as a law, you and your descendants forever"*

Reader 4: Exodus 12:25-32 (Moshe continues speaking) *"When you come to the land which Adonai will give you, as he has promised, you are to observe this ceremony. When your children ask you, 'What do you mean by this ceremony?' say, 'It is the sacrifice of Adonai's Pesach [Passover], because [Adonai] passed over the houses of the people of Isra'el in Egypt, when he killed the Egyptians but spared our houses.' "The people of Isra'el bowed their heads and worshipped. Then the people of Isra'el went and did as Adonai had ordered Moshe and Aharon—that is what they did. At midnight Adonai killed all the firstborn in the land of Egypt, from the firstborn of Pharaoh sitting on his throne to the firstborn of the prisoner in the dungeon, and all the* *firstborn of livestock. Pharaoh got up in the night, he, all his servants and all the Egyptians; and there was horrendous wailing in Egypt; for there wasn't a single house without someone dead in it. He summoned Moshe and Aharon by night and said, "Up and leave my people, both you and the people of Isra'el; and go, serve Adonai as you said. Take both your flocks and your herds, as you said; and get out of here! But bless me, too."*

Reader 5: Exodus 12:33-21 *The Egyptians pressed to send the people out of the land quickly, because they said, "Otherwise we'll all be dead!" The people took their dough before it had become leavened and wrapped their kneading bowls in their clothes on their shoulders. The people of Isra'el had done what Moshe had said—they had asked the Egyptians to give them silver and gold jewelry and clothing; and Yahweh had made the Egyptians so favorably disposed toward the people that they had let them have whatever they requested. Thus they plundered the Egyptians. The people of Isra'el traveled from Ra`amses to Sukkot, some six hundred thousand men on foot, not counting children. A mixed crowd also went up with them, as well as livestock in large numbers, both flocks and herds. They baked matzah loaves from the dough they had brought out of Egypt, since it was unleavened; because they had been driven out of Egypt without time to prepare supplies for themselves. The time the people of Isra'el lived in Egypt was 430 years. At the end of 430 years to the day, all the divisions of Yahweh left the land of Egypt. This was a night when Yahweh kept vigil to bring them out of the land of Egypt, and this same night continues to be a night when Yahweh keeps vigil for all the people of Isra'el through all their generations.*

Reader 6: Exodus 12:43-51 *Yahweh said to Moshe and Aharon, "This is the regulation for the Pesach lamb: no foreigner is to eat it. But if anyone has a slave he bought for money, when you have* *circumcised him, he may eat it. Neither a traveler nor a hired servant may eat it. It is to be eaten in one house. You are not to take any of the meat outside the house, and you are not to break any of its bones. The whole community of Isra'el is to keep it. If a foreigner staying with you wants to observe Yahweh's Pesach, all his males must be circumcised. Then he may take part and observe it; he will be like a citizen of the land. But no uncircumcised person is to eat it. The same teaching is to apply equally to the citizen and to the foreigner living among you." All the people of Isra'el did just as Yahweh had ordered Moshe and Aharon. On that very day, Yahweh brought the people of Isra'el out of the land of Egypt by their divisions.*

Reader 7: *Exodus 13:1-16 Yahweh said to Moshe, "Set aside for me all the firstborn. Whatever is first from the womb among the people of Isra'el, both of humans and of animals, belongs to me." Moshe said to the people, "Remember this day, on which you left Egypt, the abode of slavery; because Yahweh, by the strength of his hand, has brought you out of this place. Do not eat hametz. You are leaving today, in the month of Aviv. When Yahweh brings you into the land of the Kena`ani, Hitti, Emori, Hivi and Y'vusi, which he swore to your ancestors to give you, a land flowing with milk and honey, you are to observe this ceremony in this month. For seven days you are to eat matzah, and the seventh day is to be a festival for Yahweh. Matzah is to be eaten throughout the seven days; neither hametz nor leavening agents are to be seen with you throughout your territory. On that day you are to tell your son, 'It is because of what Yahweh did for me when I left Egypt.' "Moreover, it will serve you as a sign on your hand and as a reminder between your eyes, so that Yahweh's Torah may be on your lips; because with a strong hand Yahweh brought you out of Egypt. Therefore you are to observe this regulation at its proper time, year after year. When Yahweh brings you into the land of the*

Kena`ani, as he swore to you and your ancestors, and gives it to you, you are to set apart for Yahweh everything that is first from the womb. Every firstborn male animal will belong to Yahweh. Every firstborn from a donkey, you are to redeem with a lamb; but if you choose not to redeem it, you must break its neck. But from people, you are to redeem every firstborn son. When, at some future time, your son asks you, 'What is this?' then say to him, 'With a strong hand Yahweh brought us out of Egypt, out of the abode of slavery. When Pharaoh was unwilling to let us go, Yahweh killed all the firstborn males in the land of Egypt, both the firstborn of humans and the firstborn of animals. This is why I sacrifice to Yahweh any male that is first from the womb of an animal, but all the firstborn of my sons I redeem.' This will serve as a sign on your hand and at the front of a headband around your forehead that with a strong hand Yahweh brought us out of Egypt."

Leader: Traditionally, it is the children who ask four important questions that will help us understand the Exodus story. (Hand out the notecards to the children.) Parents, you are welcome to help your children if they need it!

The Four Questions:

Child One: Why is this night different from all other nights?

Leader (or another Adult): In the Bible, Yahweh has recorded through Moses the story of the departure of the Hebrew people from the land of Egypt where they had been slaves for many, many years. This night of Passover is different from all other nights, because this night is the anniversary of very last night the Hebrew people spent in Egypt. That night was very special, because Father Yahweh protected them from the last of His plagues of judgement on Egypt. That night the first-born sons of those living in the land of Egypt who did not love and obey Yahweh were struck dead. Because of this terrible event, Pharaoh (the King of Egypt) freed the Hebrew people from their slavery and sent them out of Egypt. Yahweh told the Hebrew people that they were to celebrate this special night every year forever and ever. Part of this celebration is to tell their story so we can hear it and remember all that Father Yahweh did so that they could become free men, women, and children again. He had a special plan for them too! Because of the promise Yahweh had made to Abraham, Isaac, and Jacob, He was going to give them a land of their own. In this place they could love and worship Him with all their heart. He would live there with them and make them a great nation of His Light and Truth. Through them, Yahweh would bring hope, deliverance, redemption, and blessings to the entire world.

Child Two: Why do we eat only unleavened bread?

Leader (or another Adult): The Bible tells us that the Israelites had no time to prepare to leave Egypt. Back in those ancient days, people did not buy their bread already made at a grocery store. They had to make their own bread. Nice, fluffy bread gets that way because it contains yeast. Yeast makes the bread rise and get soft. The Israelites did not have time to let their bread rise. They had to bake it without yeast, which made it flat and thick…or, if rolled very thin, hard and crisp like a cracker. Tonight we eat unleavened bread to remind us of how quickly they had to leave. When Yahweh said "Time to go!" they had to pack up and leave right away! Today, we too must always be ready to go wherever Yahweh sends us to tell others about Yeshua and His wonderful Kingdom.

Child Three: Why do we eat bitter herbs and roasted lamb?

Leader (or another Adult): On all other nights we eat all kinds of vegetables, but on this night of Passover we eat bitter herbs to remind us of the bitterness of their slavery and the bitterness of being a slave trapped in a life of sin and death. Just like our ancestors, the Israelites, we can be in slavery to the rules and traditions of men and to choices that we have made that are hurting us and others. Like Moses, Yeshua came to deliver us from the things that create bitterness and suffering in our lives and show us God's Way of living a good life in the freedom and liberty He wants for us. Just as Yahweh delivered our ancestors through the shed blood of a Passover lamb, we too find our freedom through the shed blood of the Passover Lamb that Yahweh has provided for us. That Lamb's name is Yeshua. On that first Passover in Egypt, the Hebrew people had to roast their lambs over a fire and eat it all before morning. We eat roasted lamb on this night because Yahweh instructs us to so that we will always remember what He did for them and what Yeshua has done for us.

Child Four: On other nights we usually eat our meals quickly. Why on this night do we eat our meal slowly, sitting around this special table?

Leader (or another Adult): On that first Passover our ancestors had to eat their Passover meal standing, with their shoes on and ready to go. They had to eat fast, with no leftovers, and be ready to travel a very long distance. But in the Passover celebrations every year since that night, we eat the Passover meal slowly as we remember all that Yahweh has done for us. Because this is a very special celebration, we sit at a lovely table surrounded by our family, good friends, and delicious foods. Today our lives are busy....sometimes far too busy. We eat quickly, sitting or standing – or even in our cars as we rush from one thing to another. On this night it is good for us to relax and take our time, to be with family and friends, to remember all that God has done for us, to be thankful, and to be joyful. We are a free people in Yeshua our Messiah! We are not slaves to our work or to any other man. One day, our King Yeshua will return and enjoy a Passover meal with us! This night will never be like any other night!

The Second Cup of Passover – The Cup of Plagues

Pause to be sure everyone has a small portion of wine or juice in their glass.

Leader: I now lift the Second Cup of Passover – The Cup of Plagues. The Bible tells us that Pharaoh refused to let the Israelites go, so Yahweh sent ten plagues to change his mind. We need also to remember that though the Egyptians suffered greatly under these plagues, God protected the Israelites from them. The city that they lived in, called Goshen, was a safe refuge from all that happened to Egypt.

> *"Therefore say to the children of Israel: I am YHVH; I will bring you out from under the burdens of the Egyptians, I will rescue you from their bondage, and I will redeem you with an outstretched arm and with great judgments. I will take you as My people, and I will be your God." Exodus 6.6-7*

Before we drink this Cup, we are going to names the plagues to bring them to our remembrance. Each plague sent by Yahweh was a judgment against the gods of Egypt. By condemning their gods, Yahweh made a way of rescue or deliverance for them. As we state each plague, dip one finger in your cup, and place one drop of wine/juice on your plate.

SLOWLY: Blood – Frogs – Lice – Flies – Livestock – Boils – Hail – Locusts – Darkness – Death of the Firstborn

Leader: These drops of wine also remind us of the blood Yeshua shed to deliver us from our curses. We are also reminded that there is a world out there that we need to reach with the Light and Life of our Messiah. As long as there are others our world that are in bondage, our freedom is never truly complete. We are on this earth in these days to bring the Good News of our Father's Kingdom to them so that they too can be set free. What Yeshua has done for us we also want for Israel!

Children's Activity Option: The Bag of Plagues Hand each child a Bag of Plagues. Parents help your child pull each item from the bag one at a time. As they pull them out, see if they can identify which plague that item represents. (Yes, they can take the bag and contents home with them.)

- Small packet of red beverage mix. Mix the powder into a glass of water. *The Nile turns to blood.*
- A small toy frog or gummy frog. *Frogs cover everything.*
- Rice or chocolate nonpareils candies covered with white sprinkles. *Lice infect everyone.*
- Raisins, or small plastic flies. *Flies everywhere.*
- A small toy cow, goat, horse, or camel. *The death of livestock.*
- A sheet of round stickers they can place on their arms and faces. *Boils cover the body.*
- A ping pong ball or white gumball or jawbreaker. *Hail.*
- Small toy grasshopper. *Locusts eat everything.*
- Sunglasses or a blindfold. *Darkness covers the land.*
- Small skull or skull sticker. *Death of the firstborn.*

Leader: Please join me in speaking this prayer and the blessing over The Cup of Plagues.

We thank You, Father, that because of our trust in Messiah not only are our sins washed away, but we are also protected from the curses that afflict the world around us. Not only is every curse broken, but the weeds that choke out our blessings from you have also been killed. We thank you that you make our homes like the city of Goshen: safe havens in days of troubled times. Blessed are You, Yahweh our God, King of the Universe, who creates the fruit of the vine. Amen.

Everyone drinks the Second Cup of Passover, the Cup of Plagues.

Time for a Song! This is a good place to insert a song of praise that everyone is familiar with. If there are children with you, children's songs are ideal.] Song: _____

The traditional Passover song is *Dayenu!* (Sing-along videos with lyrics can be found online.)

The Bitter Herbs

Leader: On Passover we eat bitter herbs to remember the Israelites' terrible life of slavery in Egypt for 430 years. As sweet as our life of freedom is today, let us remember the bitterness endured by the past generations for their faith in YHVH. Let us also not forget the bitterness of the lives of many of our brothers and sisters who suffer persecution around the globe right now. Place a small amount of horseradish on a bite-size portion of matzah and wait to eat this together. When we eat this, we are to let us the bitter taste bring tears to our eyes. May compassion come into our hearts for those who suffered and are suffering, as if it were us and our own families that suffer in bondage and oppression.

Please join me in speaking the blessing over the Bitter Herbs.

Blessed are You, Yahweh our God, King of the Universe, who has sanctified us and commanded us to eat bitter herbs. Amen.

Everyone eats their bitter herbs on matzah.

The Charoset

Leader: We have already dipped our parsley in salt water to remind us of our tears and we have eaten the horseradish to taste the bitterness of being in bondage. Now we will dip our matzah in sweet Charoset. Take a bite-size piece of matzah and spoon some Charoset on top. Wait for everyone to eat this together. This thick, apple and honey mixture represents the mortar our ancestors used to build Egyptian structures with the bricks they were forced to make with their own hands. Yet even in their slavery, the Israelites had hope in Yahweh that one day their Deliverer and a life of freedom would come. Today, as we face our own difficult times, the charoset reminds us that we too must always keep our hope in God. Our Deliverer has come…and he will come again!

Please join me in speaking the blessing over the Charoset.

Blessed are you, Yahweh our God, King of the Universe, who gives us hope. Amen.

Everyone eats their portion of Charoset and matzah.

The Lamb Bone

Leader: The next item of remembrance in our celebration is the Passover Lamb bone. (Hold up the shank or rib bone for everyone to see.) On Passover we eat roasted lamb – not boiled or fried. On the very first Passover, Yahweh told Moses that each Hebrew household was to select a perfect male lamb in its first year, without blemish. This lamb was sacrificed to provide a covering of protection for each home. All the blood was drained from the lamb and placed in a bowl. Then the blood of this lamb was brushed on the sides and over the door of each Hebrew home. The bowl with the remaining blood was placed on the threshold of the doorway. When Yahweh moved through the land of Egypt that night, He protected the homes of those who had listened and obeyed. As the Death Angel passed over Egypt it could not enter those homes because YHVH, our Gatekeeper, did not allow death to pass through their doors.

The meat of lamb was roasted and then had to be completely eaten. No leftovers were allowed. Anything leftover had to be burned to ashes. If a household were too small to eat an entire lamb, they were to invite neighbors to join them for the Passover meal so that the command could be fulfilled.

When the Temple was built in Jerusalem, every Hebrew man was commanded by Yahweh to travel to Jerusalem to sacrifice the family lamb and celebrate Passover. Most of the time, the man's entire family came along. Today the Jewish people no longer sacrifice a lamb on Passover because the Temple in Jerusalem was destroyed. However, they still gather in their homes and with their congregations to celebrate Yahweh's Passover to the best of their ability.

As followers of Messiah Yeshua, we know that Yeshua died as Yahweh's perfect Passover Lamb to take the punishment for our sins once and forever. Those who follow Him understand that we no longer need to make a Passover sacrifice to atone for our sin and seek YHVH's protection. Yeshua has fully supplied this for us. However, Yahweh's command to celebrate His Passover in remembrance of all He has done for us as His people still remains. On the night of His last Passover Seder on earth, Yeshua instructed us that we are to do this in remembrance of Him. We honor our perfect Passover Lamb, Yeshua, by remembering Him in our celebration.

Please join me in speaking the blessing over the Lamb Bone.

Blessed are You, Yahweh our God, King of the Universe, Who has given us Yeshua as our perfect Passover Lamb to take the punishment for our sin once and forever. Amen.

The Passover Meal

Leader: It is now time for us to enjoy the wonderful meal that has been prepared for us for this evening! Again, we are reminded that we get to slow down and savor the leisure of being free men and women. As is Hebrew practice, we will thank Father for the food after we have eaten and are full. Let's bring out our meal and enjoy!

Serve and enjoy your delicious Passover meal!
Afterwards, clear away the plates and food. *BUT be sure to leave the wine and water glasses, the matzah, some butter, a bowl of Charoset, and the Cup of Elijah.*

After the Meal

Leader: Praise Yahweh! Now that we have eaten and are full, let's thank our Father for His abundant provision. Pray with me please....

Blessed are You, Yahweh our God, King of the Universe and Creator of all kinds of foods! Father, as You have instructed us to do after we have eaten and are full, we thank you for the wonderful meal that we just enjoyed. We acknowledge and honor You as the Provider of all good things to meet our needs and bring us joy. Father, as we move on to complete our Passover Seder, we ask, Father, for your favor, healing, and blessings to rest on us. We ask that the needs that are with us around this table tonight – be they physical, financial, relational, or otherwise – be quickly met and resolved by You in the moments, hours, and days ahead. Father, may there be a double portion of blessing released over each of us tonight. We thank you in advance for all that You are about to do for us. In the name of our Messiah, Yeshua, Amen.

The Hallel (Praise)

Leader: Before we continue with the last two of the Four Cups of Passover, we have reached a time of praise! We have so much to praise our Father for! He is worthy of our praise! In Hebrew homes all over the world on this night, families sing portions of the Psalms, the Song of Moses, and other songs of worship and joy.

Stand up and stretch your legs a little! You are welcome to step back from the table so you have room to move. Be encouraged to lift your hands in praise, clap with the songs, even dance as we worship our King. Let's start by reading out loud together the opening verses of the Song of Moses followed by Psalms 113 and 114. Then we will sing a song or two of praise. Read aloud with me!

Deuteronomy 32:1-4 *Hear, oh heavens, as I speak! Listen, earth, to the words from my mouth! May my teaching fall like rain. May my speech condense like dew, like light rain on blades of grass, or showers on growing plants. For I will proclaim the name of Yahweh. Come, declare the greatness of our God! The Rock! His work is perfect, for all his ways are just. A trustworthy God who does no wrong, he is righteous and straight.*

Psalm 113 *Halleluyah! Servants of Yahweh, give praise! Give praise to the name of Yahweh! Blessed be the name of Yahweh from this moment on and forever! From sunrise until sunset Yahweh's name is to be praised. Yahweh is high above all nations, his glory above the heavens. Who is like Yahweh our God, seated in the heights, humbling himself to look on heaven and on earth. He raises the poor from the dust, lifts the needy from the rubbish heap in order to give him a place among princes, among the princes of his people. He causes the childless woman to live at home happily as a mother of children. Halleluyah!*

Psalm 114 *When Isra'el came out of Egypt, the house of Jacob from a people of foreign speech, Judah became Yahweh's sanctuary, Isra'el his domain. The sea saw this and fled; the Jordan turned back; the mountains skipped like rams, the hills like young sheep. Why is it, sea, that you flee? Why, Jordan, do you turn back? Why, mountains, do you skip like rams; and you hills like young sheep? Tremble, earth, at the presence of Yahweh, at the presence of the God of Jacob, who turned the rock into a pool of water, flint into a flowing spring.*

Time for Singing! Select one or two songs of praise that everyone is familiar with. (Song videos with lyrics can be found online. These can be extremely helpful!) Be sure to include one that the children know well.

Song #1 _____

Song #2 _____

The Afikomen and Breaking the Bread

Leader: Okay children! Remember the Afikomen – the broken piece of matzah wrapped in the napkin – that I hid earlier this evening? Who remembers what the word "Afikomen" means? ("dessert" or "what comes later") Now it is time to find the hidden Aifikomen! The one who finds the Afikomen and brings it safely back to me will receive a reward! [Give the children directions concerning finding the Aifkomen – no running, 1st floor only, etc....] Ready. Set. Go!

[While the children search, be sure that everyone's wine/juice glass has a portion for the next cup. When the victorious child returns, call the children back to their seats.]

Leader: Congratulations (child's name)! Where did you find the Afikomen? (Allow the child to answer.) Children - all of you sought diligently for this. I am proud of all of you. Each of us here this evening is wise to seek our Father Yahweh with the same enthusiasm! Those who seek Yahweh our God and find Him have found a treasure indeed! [Present the finder of the Afikomen with a reward...usually a few coins, candy, or a small toy. Instruct the children to go back to their seats. They can continue with coloring or another quiet activity.]

Leader: We've reached the portion of our Passover Seder that most Christians are quite familiar with. Churches often call this "the Lord's Supper", "Communion", or "Covenant Meal". It is my hope that tonight as we experience the Covenant Meal within the context of Passover in which Yeshua gave it to us, that we will find this blessed time more meaningful than ever before. The Covenant Meal was nothing new to the men and women with Him that evening. They had grown up with it in all the Passover Seders they had ever celebrated with their families. But this time it was going to be different. This time they would understand what the broken bread of Passover would mean for the rest of eternity. This time they would understand what the wine – the shed blood of the Passover sacrifice – would come to mean for them personally and as a people forever.

Leader: (Unwrap the Afikomen and hold it up for all to see.) Dear ones, when Yeshua celebrated His last Passover with His disciples, it was the Afikomen – this broken half of unleavened bread – which He broke and gave to them. Remember, the word "Afikomen" means "what is to come". Yeshua was about to vividly illustrate to them what He was going to for them the very next day – the day of the sacrifice of the Passover lambs. For our benefit & blessing, I am going to do as Yeshua did that evening, as recorded in Luke 22:19 - 20.

- *"taking a piece of matzah, He made the b'rakhah [blessing]."* On this Passover, I lift this broken bread before our Father in Heaven. Let us bless the bread together....

  Blessed are You, Yahweh our God, King of the Universe, who brings forth bread from the earth. Amen.

- Yeshua then *"broke it and gave it to them"*. I break off a piece of this Afikomen and give it to you. Do not eat it until we can all do so at the same time. (Give a small piece to each person or pass it around so each can break of their own piece. Use a second matzah if you need more.)

- Then Yeshua said to them, *"This is my body, which is being given for you; do this in memory of me."* Let us eat the broken bread together.

The Third Cup of Passover – The Cup of Redemption

Leader: The cup we are about to partake of is the 3rd Cup of Passover and is called the Cup of Redemption. Luke 22:20 tells us *"He did the same [made the blessing] with the cup after the meal, saying, 'This cup is the New Covenant, ratified by my blood, which is being poured out for you'."* Let this truth sink deep within you. The cup Yeshua identified as the Cup of the New Covenant ratified by His blood is this Cup … the Passover Cup of Redemption. He was telling His Hebrew disciples, "Listen! Yahweh is about to fulfill His promise to Israel that He would bring them eternal redemption. I AM that Redeemer!"

> *"Therefore say to the children of Israel: I am YHVH; I will bring you out from under the burdens of the Egyptians, I will rescue you from their bondage, and I will redeem you with an outstretched arm and with great judgments. I will take you as My people, and I will be your God."* **Exodus 6.6-7**

Before we drink this Cup, we need to understand what the New Covenant, ratified by Yeshua's blood truly is. To do this, we must look back to the promise made by Yahweh regarding what was about to happen through our Messiah's death and resurrection. Read this aloud with me.

"Here, the days are coming," says Yahweh, "when I will make a new covenant with the house of Isra'el and with the house of Y'hudah. It will not be like the covenant I made with their fathers on the day I took them by their hand and brought them out of the land of Egypt; because they, for their part, violated my covenant, even though I, for my part, was a husband to them," says Yahweh. For this is the covenant I will make with the house of Isra'el after those days," says Yahweh: "I will put my Torah within them and write it on their hearts; I will be their God, and they will be my people." **Jeremiah 31:30-33**

This is why Yeshua told the people of Israel...

Don't think that I have come to abolish the Torah or the Prophets. I have come not to abolish but to complete. Yes indeed! I tell you that until heaven and earth pass away, not so much as a yud (׳) or a stroke will pass from the Torah — not until everything that must happen has happened. So whoever disobeys the least of these mitzvot (commandments) and teaches others to do so will be called the least in the Kingdom of Heaven. But whoever obeys them and so teaches will be called great in the Kingdom of Heaven. **Matthew 5:17-19**

The New Covenant ratified by the shed blood of Yeshua the Messiah was "new" because of two big new developments in Father's complete plan of redemption.

1. No longer would we need the shed blood of sacrificed animals to atone for our sin. Yeshua was now the perfect and final sacrifice supplied by Yahweh for us to atone for our sin and make us clean in His presence. By placing our trust in Him, our sin is forgiven *and forgotten* by Yahweh.

2. In the previous covenants Yahweh had made with mankind and then with Israel, every instruction, principle, and command of God was written down on lifeless stone and sheepskin scrolls. The Covenant made with Moses and the Israelites at Mount Sinai was literally written by the finger of God on tablets of stone. This eternal Covenant was not alive and living within the people. BUT NOW the Torah – God's Instructions and Principles for a blessed life in His Kingdom – has leaped off the stone and sheepskin and is living in our hearts and minds. The very Spirit of Yahweh that gave the Torah to us now LIVES in us! His Spirit guides, instructs, and empowers us in being fully able to live in Yahweh's Kingdom NOW and forevermore. This, my friends, is the new and better Covenant of which Yeshua spoke that night!

The Torah written on stone no longer condemns any person who has placed their trust in Yeshua as Messiah. By His Spirit, the Torah journeys through life within us constantly comforting, teaching, and guiding us as we live for Him. No longer condemned and held captive by sin, we are free indeed to become all that Father has created us to be. *We have been redeemed!*

Please join me in a prayer and speaking the blessing over the Third Cup of Passover – the Cup of Redemption.

Yeshua, our Messiah and King, thank you for being not only our Deliverer but also our Redeemer. We do not take lightly the pain and suffering that you endured to shed you blood to make our redemption possible. Thank you for giving to us Your own Spirit to dwell in us as our comforter, teacher, and guide. Your love, grace and mercy given to us is beyond our small minds to grasp, yet we ask you to help us to do just that. Help us seek out and choose to follow Your Word, which is our path to an abundant life of your peace as we live in this world. Blessed are You, Yahweh our God, King of the Universe, who has given us Yeshua as our perfect Passover Lamb to take the punishment for our sins once and forever. Blessed are you, Yahweh our God, King of the Universe, who creates the fruit of the vine. Amen.

Everyone drinks the Third Cup of Passover. (And refills for the next Cup!)

The Cup of Elijah

Leader: (Pick up the Cup of Elijah.) In my hand I hold the empty cup that has been sitting on this table for us to wonder about! This is the Cup of Elijah. Yahweh's Word tells us that the coming of Messiah will be preceded by the appearance of Elijah the prophet. To this very day the Jewish people look for Elijah's return on Passover, so they set a place for him at the table and at this point in the evening open the door to welcome him.

As followers of Yeshua, we know that Yeshua told the His disciples that Elijah did come again in the person of John the Baptizer. We know that Yeshua was and is the Messiah that our Jewish brothers and sisters are looking for. We join with them in their anticipation of His soon arrival! We know that just as John the Baptizer was Elijah in Messiah's first coming, there will be another Elijah who will prepare the way for and herald His great and mighty return. Tonight, we fill Elijah's cup and open our door in our expectation of Messiah's second coming. May we also be like Elijah, making ready a way for our King and proclaiming the Good News of His Kingdom to all who will listen.

A volunteer, usually a child, opens the door while the Leader fills Elijah's Cup with wine. Also be sure that the wine glass of each person holds a portion for the next Cup.

The Fourth Cup of Passover – The Cup of Joy

Leader: We have come to the final Passover Cup– the Cup of Joy. This cup reminds us of the fourth of Yahweh's Passover promises to us.

"Therefore say to the children of Israel: I am YHVH; I will bring you out from under the burdens of the Egyptians, I will rescue you from their bondage, and I will redeem you with an outstretched arm and with great judgments. <u>I will take you as My people, and I will be your God</u>." **Exodus 6.6-7**

On the morning after the striking night of the first Passover, Yahweh took the descendants of Jacob, whom He called Israel, out of the land of Egypt and started them on a journey that would take Egypt out of them. He took them as His people and patiently, with justice and compassion, brought them to a place in their identity as a nation that He was, is, and always will be their God.

The disciple Mark tells us in his Gospel that after Yeshua and His disciples drank the third cup they sang a hymn. The hymns of Yahweh's Feasts are called HaGadol Hallel (the Great Praises) and are comprised of Psalms 113 – 118. Tonight, let's read Psalm 118 together.

Give thanks to Yahweh; for he is good, for his grace continues forever. Now let Isra'el say, "His grace continues forever."

Now let the house of Aharon say, "His grace continues forever."

Now let those who fear Adonai say, "His grace continues forever."

From my being hemmed in I called on Yah; he answered and gave me more room. With Yahweh on my side, I fear nothing - what can human beings do to me? With Yahweh on my side as my help, I will look with triumph at those who hate me.

It is better to take refuge in Yahweh than to trust in human beings; better to take refuge in Yahweh than to put one's trust in princes.

The nations all surrounded me; in the name of Yahweh I cut them down. They surrounded me on every side; in the name of Yahweh I cut them down. They surrounded me like bees but were extinguished [as quickly] as a fire in thorns; in the name of Yahweh I cut them down.

You pushed me hard to make me fall, but Yahweh helped me.

Yah is my strength and my song, and he has become my salvation.

The sound of rejoicing and victory is heard in the tents of the righteous:

"Yahweh's right hand struck powerfully! Yahweh's right hand is raised in triumph! Yahweh's right hand struck powerfully!"

I will not die; no, I will live and proclaim the great deeds of Yah!

Yah disciplined me severely, but did not hand me over to death.

Open the gates of righteousness for me; I will enter them and thank Yah. This is the gate of Adonai; the righteous can enter it.

I am thanking you because you answered me; you became my salvation. The very rock that the builders rejected has become the cornerstone! This has come from Yahweh, and in our eyes it is amazing. This is the day Yahweh has made, a day for us to rejoice and be glad.

Please, Yahweh! Save us! Please, Yahweh! Rescue us!

Blessed is he who comes in the name of Yahweh. We bless you from the house of Yahweh. Yahweh is God, and he gives us light. Join in the pilgrim festival with branches all the way to the horns of the altar.

You are my God, and I thank you. You are my God; I exalt you.

Give thanks to Yahweh; for he is good, for his grace continues forever.

Leader: Take the Fourth Cup in your right hand and focus on it. This cup Yeshua left sitting on His Passover table to remain untouched by His lips. He stated to His disciples – and to us, "I will not drink of this fruit of the vine again until the day I drink new wine with you in my Father's Kingdom." (Matthew 26:29)

What a glorious a Passover promise this is! Messiah is telling us that He will wait to partake of the Cup of Joy until He returns to be with us, His beautiful Bride, who are the people of His choosing. His joy will not be complete until that moment when we are forever His people and He our God dwelling with us again.

Family and friends gathered around this table tonight, we must each reflect a moment and ask ourselves, "Am I prepared for His return?" This is no light and passing matter. He loves us. He has done everything to make it possible for us to know Him and live in the goodness of His love, right now, in the life we have within His Kingdom every day. On that coming Day of His return, just as Israel suddenly marched out of slavery with all of Egypt's wealth to fulfill their destiny as His Kingdom in a land called Israel, at a moment's notice so we will march out from wherever we are in this world into His promised eternal Kingdom on earth. We will be fully healed, lacking nothing, and greatly blessed. We will fulfill our destiny and become His Kingdom of priests and kings. Our joy will be complete! Until then, like our Messiah we continue to endure, each of us running our race to win while we keep our focus on that great joy that is set before us.

If any of us on this special evening sense that we have lost focus, drifted off track … or maybe you have yet to enter His Kingdom by giving your life to Messiah Yeshua and making Him your Deliverer and King … then this night, the Night of His Passover, is the perfect time and season to humbly ask for and receive His forgiveness. The Kingdom is beyond measure, and all of us have opportunity step in just a little deeper year by year.

Join me now in reading aloud Hebrews 12:1-2.

So then, since we are surrounded by such a great cloud of witnesses, let us, too, put aside every impediment—that is, the sin which easily hampers our forward movement—and keep running with endurance in the contest set before us, looking to the Initiator and Completer of that trusting, Yeshua—who, in exchange for obtaining the joy set before him, endured execution on a stake as a criminal, scorning the shame, and has sat down at the right hand of the throne of God. **Hebrews 12:1-2**

Please join me in a prayer and speaking the blessing over the Third Cup of Passover – the Cup of Redemption.

Yeshua, we thank you that you held on to the joy set before you and endured death so that both your joy and ours will be complete. We thank you that you are going to return to forever dwell with us, face-to-face! We, your glorious Bride, look forward to that day with great love for you and deep longing in our hearts. Tonight, as we wait, it is our desire to manifest all the joy, goodness, and blessing that comes from knowing you as our Deliverer, Redeemer, and King. You are the One who has Sanctified us, setting us apart for your unique and uncommon calling and purposes. Forgive us, Messiah, for our sin – the things we do wrong, and the right that we fail to do, as revealed to us by your Word. We receive your forgiveness and ask for your help in being the Elijah that you have assigned us to be in this time. We thank you for the gift of the Night of Passover so that we will remember and never forget what you have done for us and have destined us to be. We are forever grateful for your Presence in our lives! Amen.

Leader: Please stand and join me in raising up the Fourth Cup of Passover - the Cup of Joy!

Everyone drinks the Fourth Cup – the Cup of Joy.

Leader: Our Seder now ends with a traditional shout that proclaims our hope for celebrating our next Passover. With joy and gusto, please join with me...for should Messiah return in the months ahead, we will celebrate Passover...

Everyone shout: **"Next year in Jerusalem!"**

A suggestion for personal or family time after the Seder:

During Yeshua's last Pesach Seder with His disciples He gave them His final teachings. These are found in the Book of John. Take some quiet time to read His words and let them fill your soul and spirit.

Following this time of teaching, Yeshua and His disciples then went to the Garden of Gethsemane at the base of the Mount of Olives. Here Yeshua spent time in intense prayer with Father in a state of deep emotional pressing. He knew the terror that He was about to face. Keeping His eye focused on the goal, He submitted His will to the Father. Shortly after His time of prayer, Yeshua was arrested and during the night hours was tried by the High Priest.

Exodus 12:42

John 13:31 – 18:27

Bonus #3:
Mashiach's Feast for Messianic Believers

As this is not a Kingdom event appointed by our King, we have no specifics instructions for our King that must be observed. All the following is based on tradition and can be used as is, reshaped to your desire, or simply serve as a guide to assist you in creating your own unique experience. The atmosphere for the evening can be as refined as you desire, or completely casual.

Preparing for the Evening

You will need:

- 2 candles and a lighter (or matches)
- Wine or juice
- A wine glass for each guest
- Leavened Bread (Traditionally, freshly baked Challah.)
- Your prepared festive meal – the family favorites are a great choice!
- Favorite hymns and songs that you will want to insert in the service given below.

Mashiach's' Feast begins after sundown on what was the final day of the Feast of Matzah, Aviv 21. Leavened foods can be brought back into the house and enjoyed. In comparison to the Passover Seder, this is a much simpler celebration that helps us bring closure to the incredible week we have experienced with our King. The Night of Passover most certainly set apart the week ahead as being different from any other week. Mashiach's Feast brings the week to an identifiable end. At sunrise, life will go back to normal and our anticipation will begin to build for Shavu'ot, the Feast of Weeks – also called Pentecost.

Invite family and friends to enjoy this lovely evening together, looking forward to the return of our Messiah and the establishment of His Throne and His Kingdom on Earth, just as it is in Heaven!

Mashiach's Feast

Welcome

Leader: Tonight, as we bring our celebration of Passover and the Feast of Unleavened Bread to a close, we want to mark the end of this sacred week in a special way. We honor our wonderful Messiah, Yeshua, who is and always will be our Passover Lamb, chosen by YHVH (Yahweh) to provide for us complete forgiveness of our sin and full entrance into His Kingdom forever. We have every hope and every confidence that Yeshua our Messiah is returning just as He promised. We have chosen to celebrate Mashiach's Feast tonight in joyful expectation of that Great Day!

To begin our special evening together, we will light the candles and share in the first three cups of the evening. Then we will enjoy a delicious meal together, after which we will share in the fourth cup of the evening and bring our week of celebration to an end.

Lighting of the Candles

The candles are lit by one of the women celebrating with you this evening.

- 1st Candle and Blessing

Blessed are You, Yahweh our God, King of the universe, who separates between the uncommon and the common, between light and darkness, between Israel and the pagan nations, and who gave us the week of Passover and Unleavened Bread for remembrance and celebration. Amen.

- 2nd Candle and Blessing

Blessed are You, Yahweh our God, King of the Universe, who was, and who is, and who is to come. Amen.

Leader: Join me as we read aloud God's Word together.

God spoke to Moshe; he said to him, "I am Yahweh. I appeared to Avraham, Yitz'chak (Isaac) and Ya`akov (Jacob) as El Shaddai, although I did not make myself known to them by my name, Yud-Heh-Vav-Heh [Yahweh, YeHoVaH]. Also with them I established my covenant to give them the land of Kena`an, the land where they wandered about and lived as foreigners. Moreover, I have heard the groaning of the people of Isra'el, whom the Egyptians are keeping in slavery; and I have remembered my covenant. Therefore, say to the people of Isra'el: 'I am Yahweh. I will free you from the forced labor of the Egyptians, rescue you from their oppression, and redeem you with an outstretched arm and with great judgments. I will take you as my people, and I will be your God. Then you will know that I am Yahweh your God, who freed you from the forced labor of the Egyptians. I will bring you into the land which I swore to give to Avraham, Yitz'chak and Ya`akov—I will give it to you as your inheritance. I am Yahweh."
Exodus 6:2-6

The 1st Cup and the Bread: The Cup of Remembrance

Leader: Our first cup this evening is the Cup of Remembrance. Let's read the Scripture together.

"I have heard the groaning of the people of Isra'el, whom the Egyptians are keeping in slavery; and I have remembered my covenant." Exodus 6: 5

"Here, the days are coming," says Yahweh, *"when I will make a new covenant with the house of Isra'el and with the house of Y'hudah. It will not be like the covenant I made with their fathers on the day I took them by their hand and brought them out of the land of Egypt; because they, for their part, violated my covenant, even though I, for my part, was a husband to them,"* says Yahweh. *"For this is the covenant I will make with the house of Isra'el after those days,"* says Yahweh: *"I will put my Torah within them and write it on their hearts; I will be their God, and they will be my people."* -- Jeremiah 31:31-33 (and Hebrews 8:10)

During this past week of celebration, we have been encouraged and comforted by the knowledge that while we have been remembering Him, He has also been remembering us! Our King is remarkable! He is kind, compassionate, patient, and just. As we close this week of Passover and the Feast of Unleavened Bread we remember and honor the Living Covenant of Yahweh who is Yeshua and who by His Spirit dwells in us.

Please tear off a piece of fresh bread and be sure your cup has some wine or juice in it.

Together let's bless the Cup of Remembrance and the Bread of His Eternal Covenant with us.

Blessed are you, Yahweh our God, King of the Universe, who creates the fruit of the vine. Blessed are you, Yahweh our God, who brings forth bread from the earth. Amen.

Everyone partakes together.

The 2nd Cup and the Bread: The Cup of Deliverance

Leader: The 2nd Cup this evening is the Cup of Deliverance. Tonight, we thank God for His deliverance in our lives. Each of us has been delivered by His mighty outstretched hand from those bondages placed on us by the world and by those of our own choosing, such as fear, anger, bitterness, rejection, dishonor, oppression, addictions, abuse…. the list seems endless and is so dark. These bondages are just as real and crippling as the bondages of slavery our ancestors endured in Egypt. To all who call on Him, Yahweh provides deliverance. His Kingdom is a realm of freedom, restoration, peace, and joy. Join me in reading these Scriptures.

"Therefore, say to the people of Isra'el: 'I am YHVH. I will free you from the forced labor of the Egyptians, rescue you from their oppression…" **Exodus 6:6**

So Yeshua said to the Judeans who had trusted him, "If you obey what I say, then you are really my talmidim (disciples), you will know the truth, and the truth will set you free." They answered, "We are the seed of Avraham and have never been slaves to anyone; so what do you mean by saying, 'You will be set free'?" Yeshua answered them, "Yes, indeed! I tell you that everyone who practices sin is a slave of sin. Now a slave does not remain with a family forever, but a son does remain with it forever. So if the Son frees you, you will really be free!" **John 8:31-36**

What is the truth that we are to know, the truth that will set us free? Let's read aloud together what David reveals to us in Psalm 119.

> *Your righteousness is eternal righteousness, and your Torah is truth. ... You are close by, YHVH; and all your mitzvot (commandments, instructions, and principles) are truth. Long ago I learned from your instruction that you established it forever. Look at my distress, and rescue me, for I do not forget your Torah.*
> **Psalm 119:142, 151-152**

Please tear off a piece of fresh bread and be sure your cup has some wine or juice in it.

Join me in speaking the blessing over the Cup of Deliverance.

> *Blessed are you, Yahweh our God, King of the Universe, who creates the fruit of the vine. Blessed are you, Yahweh our God, who brings forth bread from the earth. Amen.*

Everyone partakes together.

The 3rd Cup and the Bread: The Cup of Sanctification

Leader: Our 3rd Cup this evening is the Cup of Sanctification. What does it mean to be sanctified? The terms we often hear used to define sanctified is *to be made holy*. What does *holy* mean? *Holy* or *holiness* is not some mystical aura of profound perfection that hovers over or around a person or thing. Holiness defines the function and the character or nature of a person or thing. When something or someone is sanctified or made holy, they have been set apart to be different, uncommon, and unique – not ordinary like the usual things and people of the world. Their purpose is different. Their role in the world is different. Their destiny is different. Their mindset and lifestyle are different. Yahweh took Israel to be His People and caused them to be holy. They would forever have an uncommon purpose, role, and destiny in the earth. He calls their uniqueness *His Light*. Through the uniqueness of His people, God would speak His Truth into the nations and provide the Messiah, the One who would save all who call on Him from an eternity in darkness and death.

Like them, Yeshua calls each of us (now grafted into Israel) to be sanctified. We have been chosen, just as they were, for a different purpose, role, and destiny in the world. We are not to be like the world. We must be like Him! How we do this is taught to us by His Spirit who comforts, teaches, and guides us by renewing His Word (His Torah) in our hearts and minds. Because He instructs us through His Word, we know how to live freely in His Kingdom NOW, right where we are, no matter what is going on in the world!

Let's read these Scriptures aloud together.

"I will redeem you with an outstretched arm and with great judgments. "I will take you as my people, and I will be your God. Then you will know that I am YHVH your God, who freed you from the forced labor of the Egyptians." **Exodus 6: 6-7**

[This is Yeshua speaking to the Father in the Garden of Gethsemane the night before His death.]

"But now, I am coming to you; and I say these things while I am still in the world so that they may have my joy made complete in themselves. I have given them your Word, and the world hated them, because they do not belong to the world—just as I myself do not belong to the world.

I don't ask you to take them out of the world, but to protect them from the Evil One. They do not belong to the world, just as I do not belong to the world. Set them apart for holiness by means of the truth—your Word is truth. Just as you sent me into the world, I have sent them into the world. On their behalf I am setting myself apart for holiness, so that they too may be set apart for holiness by means of the truth.

I pray not only for these, but also for those who will trust in me because of their word, that they may all be one. Just as you, Father, are united with me and I with you, I pray that they may be united with us, so that the world may believe that you sent me. The glory [the complete presence of God's lifestyle, nature, and character] which you have given to me, I have given to them; so that they may be one, just as we are one— I united with them and you with me, so that they may be completely one, and the world thus realize that you sent me, and that you have loved them just as you have loved me." **John 17:13-23**

Please tear off a piece of fresh bread and be sure your cup has some wine or juice in it.

Join me in speaking the blessing over the Cup of Sanctification.

Blessed are you, Yahweh our God, King of the Universe, who has chosen us, sanctified us through Your Commandments and has destined us to be Your Light to the nations. Blessed are you, Yahweh our God, King of the Universe, Who creates the fruit of the vine and brings forth bread from the earth. Amen.

Everyone partakes together.

Time to enjoy Our Festive Meal!

Blessing after the Meal

Leader: Let's thank God for the wonderful meal that He provided for us. Pray with me.

> *"So you will eat and be satisfied, and you will bless YHVH your God for the good land he has given you." (Deuteronomy 8:10) Blessed are you, Yahweh our God, who provides the fruit of the earth for our use. We bless you for continually fulfilling Your promise that while the earth remains, seedtime and harvest shall not fail. Teach us to remember that it is not by bread alone that we live. Grant us evermore to feed on Him who is the True Bread from heaven, Yeshua our Messiah. Amen.*

The 4th Cup and the Bread: The Cup of Inheritance

Leader: We are about to drink the final Cup of the evening, the Cup of Inheritance. The principle of providing an inheritance for the generations that follow us is one of the key principles of God's Kingdom. An inheritance is something that is physical. It can be seen by our eye and touched by our hands. Being the good and perfect father that He is, Yahweh provides an inheritance for His People here on earth now, and again in physical form for us in our eternity with Him. Let's read together these Scriptures about our inheritance from Him.

> *"I will bring you into the land which I swore to give to Avraham, Yitz'chak and Ya`akov—I will give it to you as your inheritance. I am YHVH." Exodus 6:8*

> *"Look! I am presenting you today with, on the one hand, life and good; and on the other, death and evil—in that I am ordering you*

today to love YHVH your God, to follow his ways, and to obey his mitzvot, regulations and rulings; for if you do, you will live and increase your numbers; and YHVH your God will bless you in the land you are entering in order to take possession of it. But if your heart turns away, if you refuse to listen, if you are drawn away to prostrate yourselves before other gods and serve them; I am announcing to you today that you will certainly perish; you will not live long in the land you are crossing the Jordan to enter and possess. I call on heaven and earth to witness against you today that I have presented you with life and death, the blessing and the curse. Therefore, choose life, so that you will live, you and your descendants, loving YHVH your God, paying attention to what he says and clinging to him—for that is the purpose of your life! On this depends the length of time you will live in the land YHVH swore he would give to your ancestors Avraham, Yitz'chak and Ya`akov." **Deuteronomy 30:15-20**

Leader: The land that is our inheritance now is the land that YHVH promised to Abraham and then gave to Israel in the time of Joshua. Today, the modern state of Israel sits on only a portion of that Promised Land. Let's keep reading about our inheritance.

"Don't let yourselves be disturbed. Trust in God and trust in me. In my Father's house are many places to live. If there weren't, I would have told you; because I am going there to prepare a place for you. Since I am going and preparing a place for you, I will return to take you with me; so that where I am, you may be also.

Furthermore, you know where I'm going; and you know the way there."

T'oma said to him, "Lord, we don't know where you're going; so how can we know the way?"

192

Yeshua said, "I AM the Way—and the Truth and the Life; no one comes to the Father except through me.

Because you have known me, you will also know my Father; from now on, you do know him—in fact, you have seen him." John 14:1-7

Leader: Yeshua has a place for us to be with Him after our physical deaths until He returns with us to establish His throne in Jerusalem and restores His Kingdom on earth. Yes, for 1000 years we will be with Him in Israel. During that time, life will be on earth as it is in heaven. What was lost to us and to the earth, The Garden of Eden, will be restored. After this will be the Final Judgement and our Adversary and all who follow him – angels and humankind – will be no more. Our eternal inheritance will be bestowed. A new heaven and a new earth! Let's read these prophetic promises together.

"For, look! I create new heavens and a new earth; past things will not be remembered, they will no more come to mind. So be glad and rejoice forever in what I am creating; for look! I am making Yerushalayim a joy, and her people a delight. I will rejoice in Yerushalayim and take joy in my people. The sound of weeping will no longer be heard in it, no longer the sound of crying. No more will babies die in infancy, no more will an old man die short of his days—he who dies at a hundred will be thought young, and at less than a hundred thought cursed. They will build houses and live in them, they will plant vineyards and eat their fruit. They will not build and others live there, they will not plant and others eat; for the days of my people will be like the days of a tree, and my chosen will themselves enjoy the use of what they make. They will not toil in vain or raise children to be destroyed, for they are the seed blessed by Yahweh; and their offspring with them. Before they call, I will answer; while they are still speaking, I will hear.

The wolf and the lamb will feed together, and the lion eat straw like an ox (but the serpent—its food will be dust). They will not hurt or destroy anywhere on my holy mountain," says Yahweh. **Isaiah 65:17-25**

Then I saw a new heaven and a new earth, for the old heaven and the old earth had passed away, and the sea was no longer there. Also I saw the holy city, New Yerushalayim, coming down out of heaven from God, prepared like a bride beautifully dressed for her husband. I heard a loud voice from the throne say, "See! God's Sh'khinah (Glory) is with mankind, and he will live with them. They will be his people, and he himself, Immanu'el (God-with-them), will be their God. He will wipe away every tear from their eyes. There will no longer be any death; and there will no longer be any mourning, crying or pain; because the old order has passed away." Then the One sitting on the throne said, "Look! I am making everything new!" Also he said, "Write, 'These words are true and trustworthy!' And he said to me, "It is done! I am the 'Aleph' and the 'Tav,' the Beginning and the End. To anyone who is thirsty I myself will give water free of charge from the Fountain of Life. He who wins the victory will receive these things, and I will be his God, and he will be my son." Revelation 21:1-7

Leader: It is because of the promise of Yeshua's return and the promises of the inheritance that is being prepared for us by Yahweh, the King of the Universe, that we close this holy week of celebration with our eyes focused forward on the joy and hope that is set before us. The presence of Yeshua with us forever is our inheritance, as is the new heaven and new earth that He will one day create for us. Praise Him for His faithfulness to His People now and forever!

Please tear off a piece of fresh bread and be sure your cup has some wine or juice in it.

Join me in speaking the blessing over the Cup of Inheritance.

> *Blessed are you, Yahweh our God, King of the Universe, who has given us our Messiah Yeshua and who has chosen us to receive Your inheritance in this life and the one to come. Blessed are you, Yahweh our God, King of the Universe, who creates the fruit of the vine and brings forth bread from the earth. Amen.*

Everyone partakes together.

Leader: Please stand. Everyone, please fill your glasses one last time for the close of this holy week in this Season of Our Deliverance. (Pause.) In the Daily Prayers of the Jewish people there is a prayer for the future of Jerusalem and the coming of Messiah, the descendant of King David. We are going to close Mashiach's Feast speaking this prayer in unity with the House of Judah and in anticipation of the day when the eyes of all nations will be opened, and Judah too will know thier Messiah.

> *To Your city, Jerusalem, You shall return to with mercy, and You shall dwell in it, and as You have spoken, may You build it soon in our days for eternity, and may You establish the throne of David within it. The offspring of David your servant may You swiftly flourish and exalt his honor with Your salvation; for Your redemption we hope all day long. Blessed are You, Yahweh, who raises the ray of salvation. Amen.*

My brothers and sisters, let's raise our glasses as we say together, **"NEXT YEAR IN JERUSALEM!"**

Everyone drinks their cup. Using a drop of wine, extinguish the candles.

About the Author

Pastor Deborah Munson was born and raised in the Big Sky state of Montana. Her parents love of travel and history took her all over the USA and Europe, giving her a great appreciation for the vast beauty of God's creation and the richness of human existence throughout time. As a graduate of Crown College in Minnesota, she has been in ministry since 1980. Her ministry focuses over the years have been in Christian education for youth and adults, camp and retreat ministries, overseas outreaches, life coaching & mentoring, creative arts, writing and speaking.

Pastor Deb and her husband, Tim, have served as Christian Education directors, camp managers and program developers, associate pastors, and missionaries. They resided in Minnesota and Montana for the first 15 years of their life together. Then they lived in St Petersburg, Russia for four years (with their two daughters) encouraging pastors and strengthening evangelical churches through the Association of Christian Churches in Russia and in mission trips to Poland, Latvia, and Estonia. Returning from Russia in 1999, they made their new home in Lancaster County, Pennsylvania, where Pastor Deb founded and led a ministry to and for artists called Artists Junction.

In 2009 and 2010 her work in that ministry took her to Israel where she was confronted with the Hebrew roots of her faith in Messiah and her own Jewish heritage. Since then, Pastor Deb and her husband have dedicated themselves to studying the Tanakh (the Torah, Writings, and Prophecies that comprise the Old Testament), the teachings of the Messiah, and the letters of the Apostles from a

Hebrew perspective and within the Hebrew context through which Messiah was promised and came into the world.

The Munson's returned to Montana in September of 2011. Pastors Deb and Tim presently serve as associate pastors in the Everlasting Covenant Congregation in Billings, MT. Pastor Deb has also established Springs of Shiloh Ministries, based in their home in Shepherd, MT. This ministry focuses on publishing books and materials to help others on the same journey of restoring Biblical Hebrew roots to the Kingdom-based lifestyle found through faith in Messiah Yeshua. The ministry also takes tour groups to Israel, helping followers of the Messiah engage their faith while gaining knowledge and understanding through the Land and the eyes of the people who live there.

Pastor Deb is also a mentor, speaker, and teacher with a missionary passion! She loves to teach the gospel of the Kingdom of God wherever she has opportunity to go. Together with her husband, she has vision to establish a retreat and mentoring center in Montana, called The Springs of Shiloh. The center will allow for focused teaching and study opportunities for guests with group training and one-on-one mentoring available in adapting to a Kingdom of God lifestyle. The location will also serve those in need of a relaxing faith-based environment for rest and recharging while enjoying of the wonder of God's creation.

Though Pastor Deb's life is full of delight in pursuing the purpose and vision God has given, her greatest passion is her husband and family. She and Tim are proud parents and grandparents. These are the great loves of their life, for which they feel deeply blessed! Pastors Deb and Tim enjoy photography, painting, camping, canoeing & rafting, fishing, hiking, and bicycling in the great Montana outdoors.... always accompanied by their loyal poodle, Lady Liberty.

Want to learn more about the Biblical Hebrew-rooted faith and lifestyle of God's Kingdom?

Connect with Pastor Deb!

Pastor Deb Munson
Springs of Shiloh Ministries
springsofshiloh@gmail.com

- Website: www.springsofshiloh.com

- Facebook: "Like and "Follow" our page:
  Springs of Shiloh Ministries

- Join us on a tour of Israel! Go to our website for information on the next trip.

- Book Pastor Deb as a guest speaker. Contact her by email.

- Order resources on Amazon.com/books:
  The King's Passover
  Called to Be Men (written with Pastor Steve Heimbichner)

  … and more to come!

- Receive Springs of Shiloh email updates on new resources, upcoming projects and online classes, and opportunities to support us in the development of the Springs of Shiloh retreat facility

Made in the USA
Coppell, TX
21 March 2021